THE REFERENCE SHELF

Vol. 26   No. 5

"THE CENSORSHIP OF BOOKS"

Edited by
WALTER M. DANIELS

THE H. W. WILSON COMPANY
NEW YORK   1954

Copyright 1954

By The H. W. Wilson Company

Printed in the United States of America

Library of Congress Catalog Card No. 54-7531

PREFACE

Nobody, the compiler learned in preparing this volume, believes in censorship. Some persons would keep lurid publications and sensational comics off the newsstands and out of the hands of the young. Some would "label" or segregate in public libraries the writings of persons with subversive affiliations. Others would exclude objectionable materials from the mails and from interstate commerce.

No one, however, goes as far as to suggest prohibition of the publication of anything. The closest approach to this is found in several congressional proposals to impound the mails of persons or concerns distributing risqué or unpatriotic matter. None of these proposals, so far, has got onto the Federal statute books.

That no one believes in censorship is not to imply that no one has anything to say on the subject. Writers, editors, publishers and librarians, whose professional interests align them against any restriction on freedom of expression or learning, have much to say and, in general, say it interestingly and persuasively. Legislators, police authorities, and racial, religious, civic, professional and business groups are equally forceful in presentation of their views as to what should and what should not be permitted reading.

Among all the advocates of "controls" of one sort or another, however, it is notable that none recognize the need for any restriction on their own reading. All present themselves as the protectors of more susceptible and less discerning minds. Librarians are sometimes accused of censorship because they do not make all reading material equally available to their patrons. This criticism loses sight of the important difference between the censor's negative purpose of denying access to some material and the librarian's positive function of making available as much as possible within his space and budget limitations. The censor rejects, while the librarian selects.

It is not suggested that all arguments for "controls" are without validity. "In a changing world, where ideas move with the speed of sound and light," it is pointed out in "Censorship for the Mass Audience" in the first section of this compilation, "many feel that we must draw a line between freedom and license, that there is a clear responsibility entailed to see that ideas which reach millions are not dangerous to the welfare of the nation as a whole."

The compiler wishes to thank all writers and publishers who have permitted quotation of copyrighted materials in this volume. He is especially grateful to crusaders for various sorts of "controls" for their patient collaboration in agreeing on excerpts that fairly and adequately expressed their views.

WALTER M. DANIELS

June 1, 1954

CONTENTS

PREFACE 3

THE NATURE OF THE PROBLEM

Editor's Introduction 9
The Constitution: First Amendment 9
Mill, John Stuart. Liberty of Thought and Discussion 10
Protection or Threat? 18
Rapid Spread of Censorship .... Publishers' Weekly 23
States Tighten Controls 25
Oboler, Eli M. Congress as Censor .... Library Journal 29
Childs, Harwood L. Nature and Role of Pressure Groups 32
Bok, Curtis L. The Duty of Freedom .... Saturday Review 36
Watson, Goodwin B. Censorship and Society 39
Burke, Redmond A. The Roman Catholic Index 45

MORAL CENSORSHIP

Editor's Introduction 51
Kugelmass, J. Alvin. Smut on our Newsstands ....
.... Christian Herald 51
Fitzgerald, Thomas J. A Catholic Suggests Controls 55
The "Right to Object" .... America 57
Limits of the Right to Object 58
Malin, Patrick Murphy. The Risks of Free Speech 59
Gathings Committee Proposals 62
Patterson, W. D. Trust the People's Judgment 66
.... Saturday Review 66
Art and Prudence .... Commonweal 67

Weybright, Victor. A Publisher's Reply .... Publishers' Weekly 69

Black Samuel. A Distributor's Warning 72

Weeks, Edward A. Appeal to Booksellers .... Publishers' Weekly 74

Case, Herbert W. How Police Censors Work 76

The Issue in Youngstown .... Commonweal 78

The Threat of Vigilantes .... Christian Century 80

POLITICAL CENSORSHIP

Editor's Introduction 82

Kuhn, Irene Corbally. Book Reviewers and Communism .... American Legion Magazine 82

Hicks, Granville. Did Reds Dominate the Book Business? .... Harper's Magazine 89

Hance, Myrtle G. Proposal for Book-Labeling 96

Halpenny, Marie. Pattern for Resistance ... Library Journal 98

Eisenhower, Dwight D. The President Speaks Out .... Vital Speeches of the Day 101

Van Doren, Mark. The Book or the Author .... American Scholar 103

UNITED STATES LIBRARIES ABROAD

Editor's Introduction 107

Nerboso, Salvatore. U.S. Libraries Dispute .... Library Journal 107

Budenz, Louis F. Red Books in U.S. Libraries 111

Cousins, Norman. Why Patrons Use U.S. Information Libraries .... Saturday Review 116

Waggoner, Walter H. Purpose of Libraries Abroad .... New York Times 119

Textbooks

Editor's Introduction 121
Fine, Benjamin. How Textbooks Are Screened ....
.... Parents' Magazine 121
Lonigan, Edna. The Case Against Magruder's *American Government* .... Educational Reviewer 124
Alabama Textbook Law 126
Is Robin Hood Subversive? .... New York Times 127
Wagner, Ruth H. The UNESCO Controversy ....
.... Midland Schools 128
Varney, Harold Lord. Charges Against UNESCO ....
.... American Mercury 133
Stilwell, Clara. Textbook Pressures .... Christian Century 135
Saveth, Edward N. How to Make Textbooks "Safe" ....
.... Commentary 138
Teachers' Manifesto 142

The Censors and the Librarian

Editor's Introduction 146
Library Bill of Rights ....
.... American Library Association Bulletin 146
ALA Statement on Labeling ....
.... American Library Association Bulletin 148
The Freedom to Read .... Wilson Library Bulletin 149
Eisenhower, Dwight D. Librarians Serve Liberty ....
.... Wilson Library Bulletin 154
Lacy, Dan. Freedom and Books 155
Carlson, Oliver. Librarians' "Slanted" Guide .... Freeman 160
Earle, Elinor S. Reply to Carlson ....
.... American Library Association Bulletin 165
Beth, Loren P. The Peoria Case .... New Republic 169
Wolf, Hazel C. Solution of the Peoria Case ....
.... New Republic 172

Ulveling, Ralph A. A Policy of Limited Circulation . . . .
. . . . Library Journal 173
Taylor, Thurston. Plea for Calm Judgment . . . .
. . . . Library Journal 174
Bixler, Paul. Don't Split Collections . . . . Library Journal 175
Munn, Ralph. Segregation of Questionable Material 177
Discussion of Segregation 181
Cushman, Jerome. Citadels of Free Communication 182
Asheim, Lester. Selection vs. Censorship . . . .
. . . . Wilson Library Bulletin 186

BIBLIOGRAPHY 191

THE NATURE OF THE PROBLEM

EDITOR'S INTRODUCTION

Any discussion of censorship should start with a statement of what is to be discussed. Such a statement is given in the First Amendment to the Constitution of the United States, quoted at the opening of this section. This is followed by excerpts from John Stuart Mill's essay *On Liberty;* his exposition of the philosophical basis for freedom of expression has the same force and pertinence today that it had when written nearly a hundred years ago.

Following a general review of the background of current demands for censorship, three articles report the rapid spread of censorship in this country through direct action and police measures and through Federal and state legislation. A political scientist next discusses the social function of pressure groups and the benefits and evils arising from their activities.

A jurist who has given widely cited decisions in censorship cases points out that the right to speak has as its corollary the right and duty to listen. A professor of education discusses the effects of censorship upon public thinking and behavior. Finally, a Catholic teacher explains the restrictions upon reading imposed by the *Index of Forbidden Books* and the reasons for these regulations.

THE CONSTITUTION: FIRST AMENDMENT [1]

Congress shall make no law respecting an establishment of religion, or prohibiting the free exercise thereof, or abridging the freedom of speech or of the press, or the right of the

[1] Text from *United States Government Organization Manual,* 1952-53; revised as of July 1, 1952. Superintendent of Documents. Washington, D.C.

people peaceably to assemble and to petition the Government for a redress of grievances.

LIBERTY OF THOUGHT AND DISCUSSION [2]

Speaking generally, it is not, in constitutional countries, to be apprehended that the government, whether completely responsible to the people or not, will often attempt to control the expression of opinion, except when in doing so it makes itself the organ of the general intolerance of the public. . . .

But I deny the right of the people to exercise such coercion, either by themselves or by their government. The power itself is illegitimate. The best government has no more title to it than the worst. It is as noxious, or more noxious, when exerted in accordance with public opinion, than when in opposition to it. . . . The peculiar evil of silencing the expression of opinion is, that it is robbing the human race; posterity as well as the present generation; those who dissent from the opinion, still more than those who hold it. If the opinion is right, they are deprived of the opportunity of exchanging error for truth; if wrong, they lose, what is almost as great a benefit, the clearer perception and livelier impression of truth, produced by its collision with error. . . .

The opinion which it is attempted to suppress by authority may possibly be true. Those who desire to suppress it, of course deny its truth; but they are not infallible. . . . All silencing of discussion is an assumption of infallibility. Its condemnation may be allowed to rest on this common argument, not the worse for being common. . . .

While every one well knows himself to be fallible, few think it necessary to take any precautions against their own fallibility, or admit the supposition that any opinion of which they feel very certain, may be one of the examples of the error to which they acknowledge themselves to be liable. Absolute princes, or others who are accustomed to unlimited deference,

[2] From *On Liberty*, essay first published in 1859, by John Stuart Mill, English philosopher and economist. Text from *On Liberty; Representative Government; The Subjection of Women*. Oxford University Press. London. 1933. p5-115.

usually feel this complete confidence in their own opinions on nearly all subjects. People more happily situated, who sometimes hear their opinions disputed, and are not wholly unused to be set right when they are wrong, place the same unbounded reliance on such of their opinions as are shared by all who surround them, or to whom they habitually defer; for in proportion to a man's want of confidence in his own solitary judgment, does he usually repose, with implicit trust, on the infallibility of "the world" . . . with which he comes in contact; his party, his sect, his church, his class of society; the man may be called, by comparison, almost liberal and large-minded to whom it means anything so comprehensive as his own country or his own age. . . .

The objection likely to be made to this argument, would probably take some such form as the following. There is no greater assumption of infallibility in forbidding the propagation of error, than in any other thing which is done by public authority on its own judgment and responsibility. Judgment is given to men that they may use it. Because it may be used erroneously, are men to be told that they ought not to use it at all? . . . . We may, and must, assume our opinion to be true for the guidance of our own conduct; and it is assuming no more when we forbid bad men to pervert society by the propagation of opinions which we regard as false and pernicious.

I answer, that it is assuming very much more. There is the greatest difference between presuming an opinion to be true, because, with every opportunity for contesting it, it has not been refuted, and assuming its truth for the purpose of not permitting its refutation. Complete liberty of contradicting and disproving our opinion, is the very condition which justifies us in assuming its truth for purposes of action; and on no other terms can a being with human faculties have any rational assurance of being right. . . .

[Mankind] is capable of rectifying his mistakes by discussion and experience. Not by experience alone. There must be discussion, to show how experience is to be interpreted. Wrong opinions and practices gradually yield to fact and argument; but facts and arguments, to produce any effect on the mind, must be brought before it. Very few facts are able to tell their own story, without comments to bring out their meaning. The whole strength and value, then, of human judgment, depending on the one property, that it can be set right when it is wrong, reliance can be placed on it only when the means of setting it right are kept constantly at hand. . . .

The beliefs which we have most warrant for, have no safeguard to rest on, but a standing invitation to the whole world to prove them unfounded. If the challenge is not accepted, or is accepted and the attempt fails, we are far enough from certainty still; but we have done the best that the existing state of human reason admits of; we have neglected nothing that could give the truth a chance of reaching us: if the lists are kept open, we may hope that if there be a better truth, it will be found when the human mind is capable of receiving it; and in the meantime we may rely on having attained such approach to truth as is possible in our own day. This is the amount of certainty attainable by a fallible being, and this is the sole way of attaining it. . . .

In the present age—which has been described as "destitute of faith, but terrified at scepticism"—in which people feel sure, not so much that their opinions are true, as that they should not know what to do without them—the claims of an opinion to be protected from public attack are rested not so much on its truth, as on its importance to society. There are, it is alleged, certain beliefs, so useful, not to say indispensable to well-being, that it is as much the duty of governments to uphold those beliefs, as to protect any other of the interests of society. . . . This mode of thinking makes the justification of restraints on discussion not a question of the truth of doctrines, but of their usefulness; and flatters itself by that means to escape the responsibility of claiming to be an infallible judge of opinions. But those who thus satisfy themselves do not perceive that the assumption of infallibility is merely shifted from one point to another. . . . There is the same need of an infallible judge of opinions to decide an opinion to be noxious, as to decide it to be false, unless the opinion condemned has full opportunity of defending itself. . . .

The dictum that the truth always triumphs over persecution, is one of those pleasant falsehoods which men repeat after one another till they pass into commonplace, but which all experience refutes. History teems with instances of truth put down by persecution. If not suppressed forever, it may be thrown back for centuries. . . .

Men are not more zealous for truth than they often are for error, and a sufficient application of legal or even of social penalties will generally succeed in stopping the propagation of either. The real advantage which truth has, consists in this, that when an opinion is true, it may be extinguished once, twice, or many times, but in the course of ages there will generally be found persons to rediscover it, until some one of its reappearances falls on a time when from favorable circumstances it escapes persecution until it has made such head as to withstand all subsequent attempts to suppress it. . . .

A state of things in which a large portion of the most active and inquiring intellects find it advisable to keep the genuine principles and grounds of their convictions within their own breasts, and attempt, in what they address to the public, to fit as much as they can of their own conclusions to premises which they have internally renounced, cannot send forth the open, fearless characters, and logical, consistent intellects who once adorned the thinking world. The sort of men who can be looked for under it, are either mere conformers to commonplace, or time-servers for truth whose arguments on all great subjects are meant for their hearers, and are not those which have convinced themselves. . . .

Those in whose eyes this reticence on the part of heretics is no evil, should consider in the first place, that in consequence of it there is never any fair and thorough discussion of heretical opinions; and that such of them as could not stand such a discussion, though they may be prevented from spreading, do not disappear. But it is not the minds of heretics that are deteriorated most, by the ban placed on all inquiry which does not end in the orthodox conclusions. The greatest harm done is to those who are not heretics, and whose whole mental development is cramped, and their reason cowed, by the fear of heresy. Who can compute what the world loses in the multitude of promising intellects combined with timid characters, who dare not follow out any bold, vigorous, independent train of thought, lest it should land them in something which would admit of being considered irreligious or immoral? . . .

Let us now pass to the second division of the argument, and dismissing the supposition that any of the received opinions may be false, let us assume them to be true, and examine into the worth of the manner in which they are likely to be held, when their truth is not freely and openly canvassed. However unwillingly a person who has a strong opinion may admit the possibility that his opinion may be false, he ought to be moved by the consideration that however true it may be, if it is not fully, frequently, and fearlessly discussed, it will be held as a dead dogma, not as a living truth.

There is a class of persons . . . who think it enough if a person assents undoubtingly to what they think true, though he has no knowledge whatever of the grounds of the opinion, and could not make a tenable defense of it against the most superficial objections. Such persons, if they can once get their creed taught from authority, naturally think that no good, and some harm, comes of its being allowed to be questioned. . . . This is not knowing the truth. Truth, thus held, is but one superstition the more, accidentally clinging to the words which enunciate a truth. . . .

If the cultivation of the understanding consists in one thing more than in another, it is surely in learning the grounds of one's own opinions. Whatever people believe, on subjects on which it is of the first importance to believe rightly, they ought to be able to defend against at least the common objections. . . .

He who knows only his own side of the case, knows little of that. His reasons may be good, and no one may have been able to refute them. But if he is equally unable to refute the reasons on the opposite side; if he does not so much as know what they are, he has no ground for preferring either opinion. . . . Nor is it enough that he should hear the arguments of adversaries from his own teachers, presented as they state them, and accompanied by what they offer as refutations. This is not the way to do justice to the arguments, or bring them into real contact with his own mind. He must be able to hear them from persons who actually believe them; who defend them in earnest, and do their very utmost for them. He must know them in their most plausible and persuasive form; he must feel the whole force of the difficulty which the true view of the subject has to encounter and dispose of, else he will never really possess himself of the portion of truth which meets and removes that difficulty. . . .

To abate the force of these considerations, an enemy of free discussion may be supposed to say, that there is no necessity for mankind in general to know and understand all that can be said against or for their opinions by philosophers and theologians. . . . That it is enough if there is always somebody capable of answering them, so that nothing likely to mislead uninstructed persons remains unrefuted. . . .

Even so, the argument for free discussion is in no way weakened. For even this doctrine acknowledges that mankind ought to have a rational assurance that all objections have been satisfactorily answered; and how are they to be answered if that which requires to be answered is not spoken? or how can the answer be known to be satisfactory, if the objectors have no opportunity of showing it is unsatisfactory? . . .

We have hitherto considered only two possibilities: that the received opinion may be false, and some other opinion, consequently, true; or that, the received opinion being true, a conflict with the opposite error is essential to a clear apprehension and a deep feeling of its truth. But there is a commoner case than either of these; when the conflicting doctrines, instead of being one true and the other false, share the truth between them; and the nonconforming opinion is needed to supply the remainder of the truth, of which the received doctrine embodies only a part. Popular opinions on subjects not palpable to sense, are often true, but seldom or never the whole truth. They are a part of the truth; sometimes a greater, sometimes a smaller part, but exaggerated, distorted, and disjoined from the truths by which they ought to be accompanied and limited. Heretical opinions, on the other hand, are generally some of these suppressed and neglected truths, bursting the bonds which kept them down, and either seeking reconciliation with the truth contained in the common opinion, or fronting it as enemies, and setting themselves up, with similar exclusiveness, as the whole truth. . . .

No sober judge of human affairs will feel bound to be indignant because those who force on our notice truths which we should otherwise have overlooked, overlook some of those which we see. Rather, he will think that so long as popular truth is one-sided, it is more desirable than otherwise that unpopular truth should have one-sided asserters too; such being usually the most energetic, and the most likely to compel reluctant attention to the fragment of wisdom which they proclaim as if it were the whole . . . .

In politics . . . it is almost a commonplace, that a party of order or stability, and a party of progress or reform, are both necessary elements of a healthy state of political life; until the one or the other shall have so enlarged its mental grasp as to be a party equally of order and of progress, knowing and distinguishing what is fit to be preserved from what ought to be swept away. Each of these modes of thinking derives its utility from the deficiencies of the other; but it is in a great measure the opposition of the other that keeps each within the limits of reason and sanity. . . .

I acknowledge that the tendency of all opinions to become sectarian is not cured by the freest discussion, but is often heightened and exacerbated thereby; the truth which ought to have been, but was not, seen, being rejected all the more violently because claimed by persons regarded as opponents. But it is not on the impassioned partisan, it is on the calmer and more disinterested bystander, that this collision of opinions works its salutary effect. Not the violent conflict between parts of the truth, but the quiet suppression of half of it, is the formidable evil; there is always hope when people are forced to listen to both sides; it is when they attend only to one that errors harden into prejudices, and truth itself ceases to have the effect of truth, by being exaggerated into falsehood. And since there are few mental attributes more rare than that judicial faculty which can sit in judgment between two sides of a question, of which only one is represented by an advocate before it, truth has no chance but in proportion as every side of it, every opinion which embodies any fraction of the truth, not only finds advocates, but is so advocated as to be listened to. . . .

We have now recognized the necessity to the mental well-being of mankind (on which all their other well-being depends) of freedom of opinion, and freedom of the expression of opinion, on four distinct grounds; which we will now briefly recapitulate.

First, if any opinion is compelled to silence, that opinion may, for aught we can certainly know, be true. To deny this is to assume our own infallibility.

Secondly, though the silenced opinion be an error, it may, and very commonly does, contain a portion of truth; and since the general or prevailing opinion on any object is rarely or never the whole truth, it is only by the collision of adverse opinions that the remainder of the truth has any chance of being supplied.

Thirdly, even if the received opinion be not only true, but the whole truth; unless it is suffered to be, and actually is, vigorously and earnestly contested, it will, by most of those who receive it, be held in the manner of a prejudice, with little comprehension or feeling of its rational grounds. And not only this, but, fourthly, the meaning of the doctrine itself will be in danger of being lost, or enfeebled, and deprived of its vital effect on the character and conduct; the dogma becoming a mere formal profession, inefficacious for good, but cumbering the ground, and preventing the growth of any real and heartfelt conviction, from reason or personal experience.

Before quitting the subject of freedom of opinion, it is fit to take notice of those who say, that the free expression of all opinions should be permitted, on condition that the manner be temperate, and do not pass the bounds of fair discussion. . . . Undoubtedly the manner of asserting an opinion, even though it be a true one, may be very objectionable, and may justly incur severe censure. But the principal offenses of the kind are such as it is mostly impossible, unless by accidental self-betrayal, to bring home to conviction. . . . The worst offense of this kind which can be committed by a polemic, is to stigmatize those who hold the contrary opinion as bad or immoral men. . . . In general, opinions contrary to those commonly received can only obtain a hearing by studied moderation of language, and the most cautious avoidance of unnecessary offense, from which they hardly ever deviate even in a slight degree without losing ground: while unmeasured vituperation employed on the side of the prevailing opinion, really does deter people from professing contrary opinions, and from listening to those who profess them. For the interest, therefore, of truth and justice, it is far more important to restrain this employment of vituperative language than the other. . . . Opinion ought, in every instance, to determine its verdict by the circumstances of the individual case; condemning every one, on whichever side of the argument he places himself, in whose mode or advocacy either want of candor, or malignity, bigotry or intolerance of feeling manifest themselves, but not inferring these vices from the side which a person takes, though it be the contrary side of the question to our own; and giving merited honor to every one, whatever opinion he may hold, who has calmness to see and honesty to state what his opponents and their opinions really are, exaggerating nothing to their discredit, keeping nothing back which tells, or can be supposed to tell, in their favor. This is the real morality of public discussion.

PROTECTION OR THREAT? [3]

The radio and TV, movies, books and magazines with astronomical circulations—all these have added a new dimension to a problem that has plagued mankind since the beginning of civilization: how to deal with the obscene, the indecent, the subversive, in literature and in entertainment.

No ones likes to be called a censor, repugnant as the word is to traditional ideas of freedom of expression. But in a changing world, where ideas move with the speed of sound and light, many feel that we must draw a line between freedom and license, that there is a clear responsibility entailed to see that ideas which

[3] From "Censorship for the Mass Audience: a Protection or a Threat?" In *Platform, published by the Newsweek Club and Educational Bureaus.* p [1], 3-23. September 1953. Reprinted by permission.

reach millions are not dangerous to the welfare of the nation as a whole.

Others feel that "liberty is not a matter of arithmetic," that curbing ideas entails too great a risk to the freedom of expression that is an essential cornerstone of democratic society. Does the American public really need to be protected, they ask, and if so, what guarantees are there that the price will not be too heavy to pay?

In Congress, in Hollywood, in hundreds of city halls, in libraries and schools, churches and clubs, we are being asked daily to make decisions on the merits of individual cases. The conflict is a continuing one, the battlefield is the whole United States. . . .

As far back as the third century B. C. in the Chinese empire, the Ts'in Emperor Hwang-Ti ordered the confiscation of all the works of the past proposing to found a new society. . . . As for the public's morals, they are and long have been a major source of concern. . . . In fact, anthropologist Margaret Mead says, every known human society has made some restrictions in regard to the way in which sex is portrayed.

With the invention of the printing press, a new dimension was added. For the first time, ideas could be spread rapidly and could simultaneously reach many people in many places. And in the intervening five centuries, the size of the audience and the speed and versatility with which ideas can be disseminated have made gigantic strides. . . .

And as it became possible to spread information instantaneously to millions of people, the world was shocked into a realization of the terrifying power ideas can have. The phrase, "Ideas are weapons," is being brought home with more and more impact as the cold war progresses. . . .

In a sense, every individual exercises some form of censorship every day of his life; when he rejects one book in favor of another, turns down an invitation to see a horror movie or a sentimental love story, turns off his television set when a speaker's views infuriate him, or simply bore him. . . .

Under this all-encompassing definition, it is up to the individual to reject for himself what he finds objectionable. But in some areas, this has not been considered enough and a hodge-podge of forces is working to control the principal media of expression and to keep them within the bounds of decency and security. Broadly, there are three main avenues of control:

Laws against obscenity exist at many levels, and what is lewd may be kept from the eyes and ears of the public at various points. Customs officials may keep offending material out of the country, postal officials may keep obscene materials from being mailed, and anything which might endanger morals may be excluded from interstate commerce.

In addition, each of the forty-eight states has obscenity laws designed to deal with any obscene materials that do not fall within the range of national regulations covering the mails, interstate and foreign commerce. . . .

Still further weapons exist in many communities which have enacted local ordinances to deal with the specific material found objectionable in the community. Most of these deal with obscenity, but some extend beyond this area. An ordinance in effect in St. Cloud, Minnesota, for example, outlaws anything which is obscene or which "ridicules any person or persons because of race, creed or color; or advocates un-American or subversive activities." . . .

The movies, radio and television all operate—in varying degrees—according to the rules laid down in voluntary codes of regulation. The book and magazine industries as yet have adopted no code, preferring to depend upon what Victor Wey-bright, chairman and editor of the New American Library of World Literature, has called "the exercise of self-restraint by each individual publisher." . . .

Increasingly aware that public opinion is an effective tool for controlling expression, organized groups often take the fullest measure of advantage of their right to speak out. Almost any group with ideas it holds dear is able to protest—and does—when it feels those ideas are being offended. Thus, Jewish groups, fearful that the portrayal of Fagin in *Oliver Twist* might incite anti-Semitic feelings, were for several years able to prevent the film version from being shown in this country. Negro organizations, Elmer Rice reports in the *New Republic*

(April 13, 1953), "have repeatedly tried to prevent the exhibition of *The Birth of a Nation;* and in Southern communities, believers in white supremacy have banned films presenting the Negro in a sympathetic light." . . .

All this presents an elaborate picture of safeguards operating to keep the indecent and the subversive in practical check. On the surface, it might seem the situation is well in hand. But on the contrary, there is a conflict raging underneath all this. The controls we have set are under constant attack: there is bitter disagreement over where and how to set the limits to free expression, what sort of curbs are proper and effective, how strictly any curbs should be enforced. At each extreme, the view is that our way of life is threatened, either by too many controls, or not enough of them. . . .

The danger of subversion, this side [which advocates stricter controls] feels, is at least as demanding of attention and protective measures as the more readily identifiable dangers of indecency. As relations in the postwar years worsened between the United States and Russia, we have been faced at home with disturbing revelations which have shaken the traditional trust that is placed in the American public to choose between the politically good and bad ideas. . . .

The Government, many reason, is not the only likely target for subversives. The minds of the people are also at stake, and there is a serious obligation to see that our vast and powerful channels of communications are shut off to disloyal ideas and persons. For example, there is controversy over whether it is proper to sanction the use of communistic propaganda—open and concealed—in classrooms and libraries. . . .

And, indeed, it is not only subversive ideas, the argument continues, but any works of subversives which should be denied a free market place. Our libraries give disturbing community support to American Communists when their books are stocked. . . .

Historically, censorship, its critics argue, has simply never worked out. Nor is there any new evidence, it is further reasoned, to show that today's "dangers" are more urgent than yesterday's. Whichever way you look at it, the argument goes, there is little justification for believing that censorship is necessary, less justification for believing that it will work, and no case whatsoever for thinking that censorship can be exercised without seriously endangering the constitutional guarantees of freedom of speech and expression. Protest and persuasion are, in this view, wholly legitimate weapons against the objectionable. But to go beyond them to suppression, which prevents others from seeing and judging for themselves, is not. . . .

Attempts at suppression of objectionable material and stringent methods of advance censorship are doomed to failure, this side argues, pointing to the evidence of history as eloquent proof of this argument. . . .

Furthermore, the standards for judging may be of dubious value. Obscenity, for instance, may be measured in terms of price and availability, so that what is acceptable in royal octavo bound in cloth at three dollars is obscene in paper covers at twenty-five cents. . . . A book may be condemned for the suggestiveness of its cover, regardless of what is inside. . . .

John Stuart Mill, writing "On Liberty" in 1859, asked:

Who can compute what the world loses in the multitude of promising intellects combined with timid characters, who dare not follow out any bold, vigorous, independent train of thought, lest it should land them in something which would admit of being considered irreligious or immoral?

Any solution to the problem of censorship, Patrick Murphy Malin, executive director of the American Civil Liberties Union, has said, "is always a choice between risks. There is never a chance to make any of these choices without running into a risk on the other side of the decision which you make. . . ."

Nor does reaching a decision necessarily mean a final answer —the emphasis shifts from tighter controls to greater freedom along with the pressures of public opinion and the temper of the times. "The real question is not the freedom to read, to speak, or to be silent," Judge [Curtis] Bok has emphasized [in "The Duty of Freedom," quoted in this compilation]. "It is rather the courage to do these things."

RAPID SPREAD OF CENSORSHIP [4]

Since the recent hearings of the Gathings Committee . . . [see "Congress as Censor" in this section and excerpts from report of the Select Committee on Study of Current Pornographic Materials in the next section—Ed.] a marked increase in the number of local censorship attempts is evident. These local actions range from attempts by civic groups and organizations to call attention to the "problem" to police action in some communities to force dealers to remove certain books from newsstands. One of the most important facts about these local actions is that they sidestep judicial determination of the merits of the books.

Press coverage of the hearings was nation-wide, and a high average of lineage, editorial comment and columnists' space was devoted to the subject, most of it favorable to the Gathings Committee. And within just a few weeks of the hearings, local actions against allegedly obscene books have sprung up by the dozen. The sudden rise of local censorship actions can logically be attributed to the publicity which accompanied the committee hearings and to the implied Federal support or encouragement afforded by the committee majority's report. . . .

The epidemic of local book banning by these groups is a matter of grave concern to publishers, authors, booksellers, wholesalers and to nearly everyone concerned with the book business. Because of well-meaning but irresponsible attempts to "clean up" the distribution of reading matter, good literature is suffering the stigma of "obscenity' along with the bad. It follows that, although the paper-bound reprints and originals are under fire now, publishers of cloth-bound originals may well be encompassed by the sweeping local censorship actions.

The national extent of the censorship efforts is attested by the clippings from local papers which *Publishers' Weekly* has examined, many of them assembled by the American Book Publishers Council. In Baton Rouge, a 67-year-old news vendor was arrested; in Oklahoma City, the chief of police had ordered

[4] From "Book Censorship Is Reaching Epidemic Proportions." *Publishers' Weekly.* 163:1058-60. February 28, 1953. Reprinted by permission.

a survey of newsstands; in Huntington, West Virginia, religious leaders have met for local action; in Union City, Passaic and New Brunswick, New Jersey, police have entered the picture, inquiring into the sale of books at newsstands; in Poughkeepsie, New York, the district attorney has endorsed a rabbi's proposal for a "Clean Literature Committee"; in Akron, Ohio, the Parent-Teachers Association has brought pressure on dealers near schools; in Johnstown, Pennsylvania, the American Legion plans a "dealer cleanup."

Detroit, Michigan, and Youngstown, Ohio, are two cities where the censorship drive has gone beyond the "pressure" stage and to the courts. In Detroit, eleven firms are involved, six have been indicted and five more face indictment for "shipping banned literature." . . .

In Brooklyn [New York] sixteen candy stores in the Flatbush section have posted signs in their doors indicating that they will not sell certain books and magazines denounced by the Decent Literature Committee of Our Lady Help of Christians Roman Catholic Church. The list of "objectionable" books has been published monthly for some time by the Chicago Archdiocesan Council of Catholic Women for the National Organization for Decent Literature.

Owners of eight of the stores, according to a news story in the New York *Herald Tribune* February 19, permitted a committee "to examine and purge their stock of books." This was done, they said, to retain the patronage of the church's parishioners. The list includes comics, magazines and about two hundred paper-bound books. A spokesman for the book industry says this sort of action bans books as a favor for one group while depriving others of the availability of books they might wish to purchase. He terms it a dangerous practice which should not be allowed to spread. . . .

John O'Connor, president of Grosset and Dunlap, and chairman of the board of directors of Bantam Books, speaking before the Editors' Lunch Club, New York, on February 10, [1953] warned of the local pressures which would be exerted as a result of the Gathings Committee hearings in Washington. He emphasized that publishers must do everything they can to maintain freedom of selection, but he emphasized just as strongly that restraint must be used in the art and the sales copy on book covers, lest the badgering and local interference with book sales have the effect of forcing such restraint. He urged that publishers use ingenuity to make a book exciting instead of emphasizing incidents not representative of the book as a whole. He directed attention to the legislation which the Gathings Committee supports—to impound all mail of a firm which is the subject of a proceeding, without waiting until that firm has been found guilty!

The general picture of censorship reveals a pattern which is of concern to the entire book trade—the pattern of rapidly increasing local pressures and book banning attempts; the involvement of both paper-bound reprint and original publishers; the threat to publishers of *all* books; the wholesale condemnation of books, not judged by due process and by competent authorities but by many amateur self-appointed censors; the looming spectre of state and local legislation which would hurt the entire trade from dealer to author; and above all, the reputation of the publishing industry and the cause it serves.

STATES TIGHTEN CONTROLS [5]

In the first seven months of 1953, bills to control, penalize or change the penalties for distribution of certain types of literature were actively considered in the legislatures of the following states: Florida, Georgia, Illinois, Massachusetts, Michigan, Minnesota, New Hampshire, New Jersey, New York, Ohio, Pennsylvania, Rhode Island, Texas and Wisconsin.

Of these fourteen states, only one established this year an arm of the legislature to censor and ban books. This was the state of Georgia. . . .

Here is a state-by-state summary of legislative developments:

Florida: A bill was introduced in the House, reducing the jail sentence which could be imposed for publishing or dis-

[5] From *Review of Major Developments in State Legislatures (January-July 1953)*. American Book Publishers Council. 2 West 46th St. New York 36. Mimeographed. August 1953. p 1-5. Reprinted by permission.

tributing obscene literature from five years to six months. Sponsors said the lesser penalty would enable prosecutors to increase the number of convictions; jurors were reported reluctant to find defendants guilty and subject them to the five-year penalty. The fine possible for such an offense, however, was increased from $100 to $500 under the bill. It did not receive legislative approval.

Georgia: In February 1953, a three-man State Literature Commission was created by law and appointed by the governor. On April 10 the Commission announced a six-point yardstick by which it planned to determine whether books and magazines were "lewd" or "obscene' and therefore unfit for circulation in the state. The six points were:

(1) The publication would be judged as a whole, not in part.

(2) The central theme had to be "pornographic" to warrant the banning of a book.

(3) The intent of the writer would be considered.

(4) Channels of distribution would be examined.

(5) The age and intellectual capacities of potential readers would be taken into account.

(6) The effect on the reader would be considered. . . .

Illinois: An American Legion-sponsored bill to provide for evaluation of public school social science textbooks would have permitted any citizens to call for an evaluating committee to study any book thought to contain "un-American" or "subversive" material. The bill was opposed by Parent-Teacher Associations, the League of Women Voters, and the American Civil Liberties Union. It passed the Senate, but died in the House Education Committee.

Massachusetts: Hearings were held on two censorship bills. One would have authorized the Attorney General to appoint a citizens' committee to report to him on books and magazines they considered "obscene, lurid, depraved, and harmful to the public." The other was designed to create a decency review board to review all matters covered by sections of the state obscenity laws, and to report all violations.

Representatives of the Massachusetts Library Association, the American Civil Liberties Union, booksellers, and publishers appeared in opposition to these bills. One was finally withdrawn. The other was killed by a vote of 64 to 35 in the House.

Michigan: In April the legislature adopted a bill to tighten regulation of the sale and distribution of "obscene" literature. The measure amended existing statutes by making the provision on obscenity cover recordings and other items not previously included. Governor G. Mennen Williams signed the bill.

Minnesota: A bill was introduced in February to repeal the 1917 law covering "obscene books" and substitute more drastic legislation. The existing law made it necessary to consider the intent of the book as a whole in judging its alleged obscenity. The proposed law would have made it possible to judge a book obscene if it contained one objectionable word.

As a result of the combined efforts of the Minnesota Library Association, the local chapter of the American Civil Liberties Union, and members of the American Association of University Professors, the bill was first amended and then tabled.

New Hampshire: The Martel bill, which had been reported unfavorably by a House committee and was presumed by all observers to be dead, passed the House in a surprise action on June 3. It later passed the Senate and was signed by the governor The bill redefined the meaning of "obscene" in existing statutes to read: "As defined in this chapter the term 'obscene' shall mean . . . whose main theme or a notable part of which tends to impair or to corrupt or to deprave the moral behavior of anyone viewing or reading it."

New Jersey: The legislature passed a bill making tie-in sales of "obscene literature" with "better magazines" a violation of the disorderly conduct code. Governor Driscoll gave the bill a conditional veto, asking for an amendment to correct a technical defect. . . .

New York: Governor Dewey vetoed the Carlino bill, which extended to police chiefs and sheriffs the authority given mayors to secure court orders to seize obscene printed matter.

Ohio: Hearings were held on a bill to provide for the establishment of a censoring and licensing board with jurisdiction over magazines and small books. The measure was vigorously opposed, and did not receive legislative approval.

Pennsylvania: A bill which would have banned the sale of so-called "thrill" magazines was recommitted to committee. . . .

Rhode Island: Representative Mahoney of Woonsocket introduced a bill declaring that "the publication, sale, distribution, or possession of certain books, pamphlets, magazines or other printed papers, including comic books, is a source of crime and a basic factor in impairing the ethical development of minors and a menace to the health, safety, and morals of the youth of the state." The bill provided: "Every person who sells or distributes commercially to minors or has in his possession with intent to sell, distribute commercially, or otherwise offers for sale or commercial distribution to minors any book, pamphlet, magazine or other printed paper principally made up of pictures and specifically including comic books, devoted to the publication of fictional deeds of violent bloodshed, lust or heinous acts, shall be guilty of misdemeanor and shall be imprisoned not exceeding 2 years or be fined not exceeding $1,000 nor less than $100, or by both such fine and imprisonment."

The bill passed the House and died in the Senate Judiciary Committee.

Wisconsin: Governor Walter Kohler vetoed the Merten bill, which was designed to increase the penalties for the publication, sale or purchase of literature found by the courts to be obscene. He said:

In its zeal to eliminate such literature, the legislature has, in my judgment, imposed unreasonable penalties against persons who have committed no willful violation of the law, and may not, in fact, have known they were violating it.

The new criminal code, enacted by the 1953 legislature, provides for complete revision of the laws relating to obscene literature.

This code cannot go into effect until reviewed and reenacted by the 1955 legislature. It defines "obscenity" in language roughly embodying the rule laid down by Judge Woolsey in the

Ulysses case. [In *United States* v. *One Book Called "Ulysses,"* 1933, he held that the book as a whole did not come within the definition of obscenity that would ban its importation into the United States. His decision appears in *Federal Supplement, Cases Adjudged in the District Court of the United States.*—Ed.]

Texas: The legislature passed and the governor signed a bill which requires, as a prerequisite to adoption or purchase of any textbook, an oath by the author that he is not and never has been a member of the Communist party or a member of any organization on the Attorney General's list of subversive groups. In the event that the author "is dead or cannot be located," the publisher is required to affirm that "to the best of his knowledge and belief the author of the textbook, if he were alive or available, could truthfully execute the oath."

Three other bills affecting books in the 1953 session failed of enactment. One would have banned "lewd" books, another would have created a committee to investigate professors and books in educational institutions, and the third would have made it unlawful for schools to use any books "which seek to discredit . . . the American form of government or way of life."

CONGRESS AS CENSOR [6]

During the second session of the Eighty-second Congress, a total of 4,549 measures were introduced. Of these only a very few concerned librarians who are becoming increasingly aware of the postwar censorship that is seemingly inevitably descending upon us. A total of less than ten bills and resolutions from more than 4,500 possibilities would seem like a not too worrisome proportion. Yet the danger in these censorship measures far exceeds their insignificant number.

Congressional activity aimed at books and libraries began only a few weeks after the solons assembled. On January 30, 1952, Representative Harold Velde (Republican, Illinois) offered H.R. 6335, "a bill to provide that the Librarian of Congress

[6] From an article by Eli M. Oboler, librarian, Idaho State College Library. *Library Journal.* 77:1927-30. November 15, 1952. Reprinted by permission.

shall mark all subversive matter in the Library of Congress and compile a list thereof for the guidance of other libraries in the United States." This bill was referred to the Committee on House Administration and was never reported out. In a strongly worded editorial which appeared on February 24, the New York *Times* described the task proposed for the Librarian of Congress as "a presumptuous one to undertake in a society where freedom of choice in most things has been one of the cardinal tenets of a successful way of life." The *Times* felt that "it would be no different from what is being done in totalitarian countries, where so little faith is held in the people's ability to discriminate that it is felt necessary to bar all possible avenues for deviation." The editorial concluded: "The bill itself is not so much a matter of concern as is the thinking which prompted it. Fear has allowed good sense to be tossed out of the window, to be replaced by a jittery tension which demands authoritarian action. Fear of communism is justified, but communism cannot be fought by going into hiding. The battle must be fought with full knowledge of what is being fought."

Representative Velde is a former FBI agent and a member of both the House Un-American Activities Committee and the House Education and Labor Committee.

Representative Ernest K. Bramblett (Republican, California) introduced H.R. 6523 on February 11. This was "a bill to prohibit the transmittal of communistic propaganda matter in the United States mails or in interstate commerce for circulation or use in public schools." . . . Any individual or organization violating this rule would . . . be guilty of a felony punishable by five years' imprisonment and $10,000 fine.

Emerging victorious in a scramble among several legislators who wished to be in charge of a congressional investigation into the state of morals in our literature, Representative Ezekiel C. Gathings (Democrat, Arkansas) was appointed on July 2 as chairman of a "Select Committee on Study of Current Pornographic Materials." . . .

During debate on this resolution on May 12, Representative Chet Holifield (Democrat, California) stressed that . . . [the members of the committee] "will have a hard time writing legislation which will protect the people from literature which they may think undesirable but which, if attempts are made to legislate against it, they may find that it will have an overlapping effect upon the privileges of free speech and free press." Representative Eugene J. McCarthy (Democrat, Minnesota) warned that "when government goes to extremes, the effect is to violate fundamentally the right of the individual and person to think for himself and to choose for himself." . . .

On May 9, the House of Representatives passed H.R. 5850, "an Act to authorize the Postmaster General to impound mail in certain cases." Representative Tom Murray (Democrat, Tennessee) was the bill's sponsor. Although approved by the Senate Committee on Post Office and Civil Service on July 3, the bill failed to pass in the Senate, mainly because of objections by Senator George Smathers, (Democrat, Florida) and Senator Herbert Lehman (Democrat, New York). Senator Lehman quoted one of his constituents as saying: " . . . if the Department independently determines that a book is obscene, and institutes proper administrative proceedings, all mail addressed to the publisher may be impounded until final decision of the issues, which may be a matter of years, and which may ultimately establish that the book is in fact not obscene. . . . This is in fact the power to control the industry by precensorship in violation of the Bill of Rights and of the basic tenets of our democracy."

Another bill proposing to use the United States Post Office as a punitive agent was H.R. 7434, presented by Representative Abraham Multer (Democrat, New York) on April 7. This bill was aimed to bar from the mails "all papers, pamphlets, magazines, periodicals, books, pictures, and writings of any kind containing any defamatory and false statements which tend to expose persons designated, identified, or characterized therein by race or religion, any of whom reside in the United States, to hatred, contempt, ridicule, or obloquy, or tend to cause such persons to be shamed or avoided or to be injured in their business or occupation. . . . " It is specifically left to "the court" to determine whether the matter . . . "is in fact defamatory and false." The bill was pigeonholed by the House Committee on Post Office and Civil Service.

NATURE AND ROLE OF PRESSURE GROUPS [7]

Libraries, in company with other public institutions, live in an environment of pressure groups; that is, in the midst of groups of people seeking to influence the attitudes, opinions, and behavior of others. These groups vary greatly in size, aims, methods, resources, and in their impact on society. There are powerful economic organizations such as federations of farmers, labor unions, trade associations, and chambers of commerce. There are medical societies, religious denominations, women's associations, veterans' organizations, patriotic societies, and others too numerous to mention. They function on the state and local as well as the national and international level. Their number is legion. They may be found anywhere and everywhere. Some have aims as broad as a political party platform. Others stress more specialized goals such as prison reform, the single tax, prohibition, civil service reform, and the like. Our community and national life is what it is largely because of the activities of these groups.

Pressure groups have been subjected to a great deal of criticism, so much in fact that the term itself often seems to have an evil connotation. Almost every aspect of group existence has been challenged at one time or another—for example, the group objectives, the methods used to exert influence, the lack of organizational democracy, the sources and extent of group power. In the face of so much criticism it is important to remember that pressure groups in general have arisen because they satisfy some social need, that they perform useful as well as objectionable functions, that they are an integral as well as an indispensable part of the community. If, from our personal point of view, the aims of some groups are pernicious; if they employ methods which are objectionable; if they are undemocratic; or if they seem to exert more influence than they should, care must be

[7] From "Pressure Groups and Intellectual Freedom," by Harwood L. Childs, professor of politics, Princeton University, In *Freedom of Communication;* proceedings of the First Conference on Intellectual Freedom, New York City, June 28-29, 1952; edited by William Dix and Paul Bixler. American Library Association. Chicago. 1954. p73-87. Reprinted by permission.

taken to keep the over-all pressure group picture in perspective. Shortcomings must not overshadow and obliterate the good.

What services do pressure groups render? Their role is to help the public generally and government officials particularly to formulate public policy. They perform many other functions, of course. But the principal reason for granting groups of people the right of association and freedom to express their opinions is the conviction that such freedom to advocate ideas, such competition for public support and governmental approval, are best calculated to insure an enlightened public opinion and wise public policy. The American theory of government rejects the authoritarian notion of government by dictators, philosopher guardians, aristocratic, oligarchic, or any other type of elite. It places its confidence in people, in their ability, based on native intelligence buttressed by education and information, to choose their principal governmental officials, to define the ends of public policy, and to assist their official representatives by advice and the free expression of opinions. Pressure groups make their greatest contribution to the democratic process by taking an active part in the great competitive arena of ideas, expressions of opinion, and, if you wish, propaganda. The more the participants the keener the intellectual competition, the greater the variety in points of view, the more cogent the arguments, the more abundant the evidence, the greater the likelihood that the public and their chosen representatives will formulate wise public policies. . . .

In view of this . . . list of valuable services performed, what are the evils, if any, of pressure group activity? Why is their existence maligned? Why are they so passionately damned by leaders everywhere? Many claim, and this is perhaps the most frequent charge against them, that some groups exert more influence than they should. Labor leaders attempt to pin the label of "undue influence" on business groups, and business groups reply in kind. Little farmers attack big farmers with the same cudgel. The American Legion, the American Medical Association, the National Electric Light Association, the Anti-Saloon League, the Liberty League, groups of real estate men, the oleomargarine interests, the China lobby—in fact, most if not all of the more important pressure groups—have been subjected to this criticism at one time or another. Nearly everyone would agree that it is undesirable for groups to exert on government or on any other institution undue influence. But how much influence do they exert? And even more important, what is a fair amount of influence for a group to exert? Efforts to measure the influence of specific groups have not been too successful. To be sure, groups seldom hesitate to claim credit for such results as the passage of legislation, but the multiplicity of influences which combine to produce a specific effect such as the passage of a law are so confused and indeterminate that precise statements of cause and effect are often very difficult.

Even more difficult is the question of what influence a group should exert. Should it be in proportion to the size of the group, the quality of the membership, the excellence of group objectives, or what? Specifically, should a labor union with one million members have ten times the influence of an employer association with 100,000 members? Is the Red Cross, because of its aims, entitled to more influence than a national association of race track owners? Is the American Chemical Society, because of the intellectual attainments of its members, entitled to more influence than a federation of comic book publishers? In a sense these are academic questions, as all difficult questions usually are labeled. But they are also very practical and extremely important. Certainly we are in no position to say what that influence should be. The American theory of government tends to avoid a direct answer. Instead of assigning specific degrees of influence to different groups, it merely assumes that if they compete freely for public support according to prescribed rules of the game, then the truth—in the sense of the wisest view—will win out, regardless of the size, material resources, or other aspects of the group advocating the view. This is, of course, a very big assumption. Even in courts of law where much more attention has been given to devising rules that would ensure the victory of reason over emotion, other factors than the pure, intellectual merits of propositions now and then win out. In the court of public opinion very few rules to safeguard the nature of pressure group competition exist.

A second criticism of pressure groups alleges the employment of reprehensible tactics and strategies. The basic reason why pressure groups are a menace, according to some, is not the influence exerted by the group, but the way it seeks to obtain that influence. This allegation undoubtedly goes to the very heart of the pressure group problem. The American theory of government is definitely committed to the view that any and every group should have the right to propagate its ideas, to express its opinions freely, provided it does so in a way which does not do violence to the assumptions underlying the truth and market place theory. For example, so-called patriotic groups have every right to advocate the removal of Marxist or free love literature from library shelves. So long as they seek to present their views in a proper manner, they are performing a needed and desirable function in the democratic process. But what is a proper manner? When does socially desirable argument and persuasion become pernicious pressure?

It is not too difficult to give the answer in general terms. The difficulties arise in application. Since the primary objective of pressure group competition is to enlighten the public and assist public officials to arrive at wise policy decisions, methods which contribute to these ends are desirable; those which do not are a menace. In other words, propaganda and pressure methods which make it more difficult for the public and the government to decide wisely, which substitute threats for reason, which use promises of special favor in place of evidence, which deceive, distract, confuse, and otherwise defeat the purpose of pressure group competition are not proper according to democratic theory. Although there will be cases where it will be extremely difficult to decide whether the method is or is not pernicious, in the great majority of instances the decision will not be too difficult.

The community as a whole, in contrast to the particular pressure group, is not interested in the victory of any particular group at any cost. It is merely interested in seeing to it that success goes to the group with the wisest policies rather than with the most money or the fewest ethical qualms. Already many of the cruder forms of undesirable pressure such as outright bribery, libel, slander, and force have been outlawed. In certain sectors of the pressure group battle still further checks have been imposed by the government through corrupt practice acts, the Federal Trade Commission, and other agencies. Also, in some fields such as radio broadcasting, motion pictures, the press, and trade associations, efforts to curb undesirable practices have been made by private individuals and groups. The problem is to ensure the continuance of a competitive arena in which the rules of the game make it easier for appeals to the intellect, unselfish devotion to the public interest, and wisdom rather than foolishness to survive. It is a problem of raising the level of pressure group competition without infringing upon the freedom to advocate particular points of view. Ideas must be free; methods of advocating ideas must be consistent with the democratic thesis.

THE DUTY OF FREEDOM [8]

Behind our freedom to read is the freedom of others to speak and to write. Legally, these freedoms are at a high point: any blatancy, however strident, is protected; and the temper of the times is such that, at least in the field of the written word, obscenity, blasphemy, public criticism, and general outcry go relatively unscathed.

At the same time the freedom of silence is at a low ebb. If challenged, or if seeking public employment, no person may safely refuse to state his loyalty, and it is the temper of the times to regard silence on this subject either as suspicious or as fatal to man's desire to serve his community. This is nothing new in itself, since the refusal to speak required words has cost the lives of many people, from Jesus down through the saints and martyrs.

What gives the subject a fresh twist is that the suppression of silence, hitherto a weapon of tyrants, should make headway in a nation founded upon freedom of conscience. It is incredible that any part of American freedom should be considered weaker than the dangers that confront the country. Principles considered good enough to live by should be considered good enough

[8] From an article by Curtis L. Bok, judge of the Superior Court of Pennsylvania. *Saturday Review.* 36:27-8. July 11, 1953. Reprinted by permission.

to die for, if it comes to that. Since it hasn't come fully to that, we must be in a phase when weakness is being experimented with, as it was in Germany during the thirties. . . .

Our Anglo-Saxon system of law is not considered divinely inspired except as it reflects the best faith and conscience of those who live by it. It may therefore be regarded as an anvil on which we hammer out our social experiments, like prohibition, censorship, and ideological conformity. Behind the anvil is the force of public opinion, the real censor who controls our freedom to read, to be spoken to, and to be silent.

When I say that I believe in censorship, I trust you will read on. The following things are forms of censorship in which one may believe to greater or lesser extent: the general idea of law and order, the penal and civil codes, the tax law, Emily Post, custom and habit, conscience, religion, and the editorial process—not necessarily in that order. At the bottom of the list stand a few pale and timid moral laws, some of which become energized on rare occasions by the First Amendment to the Constitution. This amendment compels us, if we think about it, to speak freely and fully, or answer for it. Nothing less than the whole truth will do, in the long run, provided it be in fact the truth; but the full light of the First Amendment becomes a bit embarrassing when turned upon some of the darker corners of our living. The trouble is not with free speech but with free truth, and this may be one reason why a book that has become a classic has little to fear from the law. Two things have happened to it: it has been accepted as truth, and perhaps on that account it has ceased to be interesting. We think we love truth more than we actually do.

Truth has a way of shifting under pressure. If you must know what truth is, Holmes said that it was what he couldn't help thinking, with the surmise that his "can't helps" were not necessarily cosmic. It is largely a matter of what agitates society at the moment, for while men are always on fire over their opinions, they are rarely so on more than one front at a time. For a long time the front was religious heresy, then it was political nonconformity, then it was sexual immorality, and recently it has swung to treason. Primary attention just now does not focus on heresy, political independence, or immorality so long as we are concerned with annihilation by the hydrogen bomb.

The real question is not the freedom to read, to speak, or to be silent. It is rather the courage to do these things. The legal freedoms exist, but now and then a price is put upon them. And it is the price that effectively destroys the freedom, people being what they are. This can be vicious, for the freedoms ostensibly remain. So long as a man howl with the wolves, he may say whatever monstrous thing occurs to him; if he howls against the wolves, it may cost him his job, his social position, and perhaps his liberty. Free speech is at a minimum in the areas of the fighting faiths.

The reading public has little to fear at present from the legal censor. Last December a congressional committee [see excerpts from Gathings committee report in the next section—Ed.] published its report on pornographic material. It found that an appalling amount of it exists, mostly in little books. The committee's conclusions are interesting. They begin with the statement that the members had found it necessary during the hearings to make public announcements that the very idea of censorship was as repugnant to them as it was to the publishing industry. . . .

It is not legal censorship that I believe in but the kind that exists in every person and flowers best in the free air of competitive discussion. It forwards the development of taste, and in the public market no holds need be barred. Justice Brandeis said in the case of *Whitney* v. *California*: "No danger flowing from speech can be deemed clear and present unless the incidence of the evil apprehended is so imminent that it may befall before there is opportunity for full discussion." It is hard to see how obscene speech could result in danger before the community had a chance to answer back. The public has been answering back since the time when Plato said that Homer should be expurgated before Greek children should be allowed to read him. . . .

For almost a hundred years after the Revolution we got along without laws on the subject. Suppression has been a phase. Today the consensus of preference is for disclosure rather than stealth, and that in itself is a moral code. The present public attitude is that of the thoughtful gentleman who invented an eleven-foot pole so he could touch all the things he wouldn't touch with a ten-foot pole. Hence I believe in the censorship of the open market rather than of the police station. A ban keeps up both the demand and the profits: when the market is open the demand seals itself off and is limited to the sick in mind and spirit who will be with us until we become wise enough to heal them.

Above the bare legal right to speak or to read is the courage to use these rights well: to speak clearly, bravely, and accurately, and to read with understanding. On the other side is the right to maintain a lighted silence, and this right must still be fought for. . . .

The freedom to read does not mean the right to sit by the fire with a book. It means the right to listen to a free voice speaking from the page, the right of that voice to speak fully to our condition, and our right to reply in freedom or to remain quiet if we will.

CENSORSHIP AND SOCIETY [9]

All that will be attempted in this paper is to propose some hypotheses about censorship which appear plausible in the light of what is now known in the science of human relations. The fifteen propositions which follow will have served the purposes of this conference if they contribute some insight into factors which should be more seriously considered by law-making, law-interpreting and law-enforcing agencies. The first three are directed at the setting which fosters censorship.

1. The first hypothesis is that censorship arises out of the insecurity of a society. This hypothesis, and most of the others apply equally whether the censoring agency be government, church, business or minority pressure group. . . .

[9] From "Some Effects of Censorship Upon Society," by Goodwin B. Watson, professor of education, Teachers College, Columbia University. In *Social Meaning of Legal Concepts; no5, Protection of Public Morals Through Censorship*, collected papers read at annual conference conducted by New York University School of Law, 1952, edited by Bernard Schwartz. p73-86. Reprinted by permission.

So long as the powers that be, along with the established mores, taboos, and status distinctions of the culture are accepted without serious question, there is no need for controls to keep deviates in line. When power hangs in the balance, what the rulers fear is not so much doctrine as defiance. The laws may be framed against evil, but the machinery is set to catch devils or those who have consorted with devils. Oaths, tests and a bowed knee are required. . . .

2. The second hypothesis follows from the first: Censorship, for the protection of public morals, is applied to controversial matters upon which convictions, tastes and judgments differ. Although the advocates of any "ban" like to maintain that it is supported by "all decent and right-thinking people," this is rarely true. Wartime censorship of matter which might be helpful to the enemy is about the only case in which public opinion approaches unanimity. Censorship is coercion of the opposition. It is the imposition of the view of the authorities upon persons still persuaded of a contrary view. Milton in his *Areopagitica* warns that, under censorship, truth is one of the first casualties. . . .

3. As our third hypothesis, we note that the demand for censorship very seldom comes from persons who wish their own morals protected. Censorship commonly represents the White Soul's Burden. The arbiters of other people's morals say, in effect, "We are clearly able to distinguish right from wrong and to resist our lower impulses, but the rest of mankind is weak and needs us to shield them from awe of temptation.". . .
It might be an interesting innovation if censorship laws operated only when a plaintiff could prove that he himself had been depraved for lack of proper public safeguards.

Our first three hypotheses thus give us a picture of the demand for censorship as arising out of a situation of social insecurity in which some group, very sure of its own virtue and wisdom and wishing to establish its power, endeavors to compel persons of different mind to submit and to conform.

4. A review of censorship operations in many times and places suggests that its advocates have exaggerated expectations of the effectiveness of a legal ban. Actually, censorship rarely

succeeds in its effort to keep the disapproved material out of circulation. Those who believe in or desire to disseminate or to receive the contraband, are ingenious in devising ways to outwit the censor. "Every censorship," according to Harold Lasswell, "produces a technique of evasion as well as a technique of administration." . . .

Repression does not ordinarily annihilate the expressions of dissenters; it serves only to drive these into underground channels. In many situations the influence from illegitimate sources outweighs that from open and above-board propaganda. "Inside dope," by quiet word of mouth from another child, may quite possibly undermine all the public propaganda from parents and department stores about Santa Claus. Brazil outlawed communism in 1947, but reports indicate substantial growth of that party during its five years of illegal operation. Censorship commonly determines along what pathways the forbidden material may move—not whether or not it shall circulate. Censorship may, as we shall propose in our next hypothesis, even increase that circulation.

5. Hypothesis five is the familiar proverb that forbidden fruits are sweet. Edmund Wilson's *Memoirs of Hecate County* might have counted upon a normal sale of perhaps five thousand copies. After the vice squads seized it and before the final court order, some seventy thousand copies were sold. [Edmund Wilson's *Memoirs of Hecate County* was adjudged obscene by the Supreme Court in 1948.—Ed.] Publishers are sometimes accused of trying to get a book banned in Boston so that readers everywhere—including Boston—will want to find out for themselves how terrible it is. . . . Young people, struggling in the perennial adolescent rebellion against parents, are particularly susceptible to the lure of secret exploration of mysteries adults have tabooed.

6. Our sixth hypothesis is that knowledge of censorship introduces a debasing distortion in the way an object is thereafter perceived. A book, magazine, film, painting or letter which is known to have been banned, as a whole or in part, is approached with curiosity focused upon its wickedness. . . .

7. Our seventh hypothesis is that the most effective censorship is that which goes unrecognized. . . . "Anonymous authority," says Erich Fromm (in *Escape from Freedom*), "is more effective than overt authority, since one never suspects that there is any order which one is expected to follow." . . . Morris Ernst (in *The First Freedom*) concludes that, "Far more is kept from our minds by lack of diversity of ownership of the means of communication than by government interference." An important reason for public docility under totalitarian regimes is that when all channels of communication come under single control, people have no way of becoming aware what they are missing.

8. Some important consequences flow from the fact that those who are especially vigilant in any form of heresy hunting are predominantly persons who are themselves emotionally disturbed. . . . Such personality studies as have been made reveal that the conscious desire of agitators to serve religious, moral and patriotic ends is reinforced by powerful unconscious drives. . . . However moderately and temperately a law may be drawn, its enforcement will come into the hands of the intemperate. They are the ones who care. Every period when censorship runs high reveals inquisitors who find suspicious tongues in trees, forbidden books in the running brooks, suggestive symbols in stones and bad in everything. . . .

9. The "masses," even in the United States of America, still are predominantly authoritarian in basic personality attitudes. They want and expect to be told by parents, teachers, priests, officials, Dorothy Dix, H. V. Kaltenborn, and Mr. Anthony what is right and what is wrong. As social psychologists in recent years have studied the phenomenon of dictatorship, they have come to give increasing weight to the craving of many persons to submit completely to what they regard as a wise, just, and powerful authority. . . .

Tolerance is never very widespread, and in times of special patriotic fervor or mass hysteria people seem to release a tremendous store of accumulated hostility in attacks on unbelievers, outcasts, witches, lynch victims, sex fiends, foreigners, radicals, subversives and other scapegoats. It is only a small minority in any nation which can contemplate the possibility that it may be mistaken even in that which appears most self-evident. . . .

From the widespread popular demand, in times of tension, for repressive thought control (Hypothesis 9), and the peculiarities of the censor-prone personalities who enforce such controls (Hypothesis 8) we can deduce that it will be difficult to set rational limits to censorship. There follows our tenth hypothesis.

10. The area covered by a prohibition tends inevitably to spread.

Behind every taboo lie popular passions. The definition of what is forbidden can never be sharp enough to give citizens assurance. Around the umbra of black acts spreads a penumbra of shadow merging imperceptibly with the light of approval. . . .

Even though in its strictly legal form censorship be limited to a few extraordinarily offensive or heinous activities, the pressures generated within an atmosphere of insecurity and social tension, when applied by personalities who get gratification from espionage and persecution, tend to diffuse fear throughout the entire population. Underlying theological . . . or ideological controversies, there is usually a power-struggle and the real aim is not to find truth, beauty or goodness, but to win at any cost. . . .

11. Authoritarian domination creates public apathy. "Liberty," said Milton, "is the nurse of all great wits." Close supervision of the arts in Fascist Italy, Nazi Germany and Soviet Russia reduced the quality of painting, drama and novel to stereotyped propaganda.

There is in social science a principle of self-justifying expectations. The presupposition of censorship is that citizens are unable to judge rightly for themselves. . . . When it is presumed that people are incompetent and dependent, they are treated in ways which further decrease their competence and increase their dependence upon governing authority. Where censorship has long been thorough, public capacity for independent judgment declines. . . .

Our twelfth hypothesis proposes that the case for censorship to shelter children and youth also rests upon psychological fallacies.

12. The character and the tastes of youth are better formed by guidance than by protection. The public has an exaggerated notion of the susceptibility of children to immoral suggestions. Any parent or teacher can furnish striking evidence that children are frequently quite uninfluenced by exhortations which are dinned into them day after day from the most reputable sources. . . . What innocent children most need is not a sterile environment from which all evidence of birth, lust, violence, disease, prejudice, crime, and death has been removed, but help in interpreting the evil which is an inescapable part of life. Home, school and church should cooperate not to create an artificial, hothouse insulation from life's realities but to enable children to respond, "Ah yes! I understand." . . .

This discussion of the effects of censorship upon society would not be complete without some attention to the effects of the absence of censorship upon society. Our three hypotheses about freedom cannot yet be validated because the world has never seen any nation free for a long time of "every form of tyranny over the mind of man."

13. Some excess may be anticipated in the first reaction to liberation. Experiments in the removal of controls in boys' clubs, group therapy, or classrooms, and the record of abolition of slavery and of Prohibition support an hypothesis that the lifting of a ban brings a temporary upsurge of wild, unrestrained indulgence, which after a time subsides. Self control replaces external control and offensive behavior may drop to a level even below that which prevailed under conditions of censorship.

14. A second hypothesis on freedom is that when coercion is abandoned, efforts at education, guidance and persuasion increase. If magazines, movies and television programs were quite uncensored and diverse, parents and teachers would take more active responsibility for helping children develop standards of taste and discrimination.

15. Finally, our fifteenth hypothesis asserts that the principle of self-justifying expectations operates also under freedom. People treated as if they were able to decide wisely for themselves become so.

The conclusion that even small children have a considerable capacity for healthy self-regulation is supported by recent experiments in self-demand schedules for infants and self-chosen diets for young children. Good teachers no longer teach reading by a rigid calendar, but begin when something called "reading readiness" appears. Pupils free to choose their own curriculum seem to learn even the traditional requirements better than they do when these are prescribed for them. . . . Given support and understanding, but no direction or advice, individuals move demonstrably in the direction of more respect for themselves, more appreciation of others, better foresight, planning and responsibility.

The basic hypothesis of freedom was effectively stated by the Chinese sage Lao-tzu twenty five hundred years ago.

A sensible man says:

> If I keep from meddling with people, they
> take care of themselves,
> If I keep from commanding people, they
> behave themselves,
> If I keep from preaching at people, they
> improve themselves,
> If I keep from imposing on people, they
> become themselves.

THE ROMAN CATHOLIC INDEX [10]

A Catholic lives by faith. His every purpose, his every action flows from faith. This faith is based not on reason alone, but on reason enlightened by divine revelation. The Church is the custodian of divine revelation and, therefore, it is her duty to interpret the teachings of Christ. It is the acceptance of this fact which supports the whole structure of the Church's control of literature. . . .

[10] From *What Is the Index?* by the Reverend Redmond A. Burke, librarian, De Paul University. Bruce Publishing Company. Milwaukee, Wisconsin. 1952. p 1-9, 15-24, 32-8, 42-3, 46-9. Reprinted by permission.

The Catholic Church has always had great respect for books. She has been concerned not only with books on the liturgy, but with secular literature as well. She is, therefore, conscious of a twofold duty: to sponsor the reading of good books and to discourage the reading of those works endangering faith and morals. . . .

The present literary policy of the Church may be considered in three classifications: (1) Prior censorship, the examination of books on their moral and doctrinal aspects before publication. (2) Prohibition of books, including the methods to be used in examining a book dangerous to right faith or morals, which serves as an auxiliary to the general definitions of harmful works. (3) The penalties assessed against violators of these regulations. . . .

The opening canon on book regulations [canon 1384] states the right and the obligation of the Church to control literature, saying:

> The Church has the duty to demand that Catholics shall not publish books which she has not examined in advance. She has also the right to forbid for a just reason books published by others. . . .

As implied by the canon, the Church has the duty of preserving the deposit of faith, and one means of doing this is to examine and censor books on faith and morals before their publication, and to condemn harmful books already published. . . . Vast fields of literature, such as fiction, poetry, and drama, generally do not need ecclesiastical approbation, although some may not be read because of their violation of moral principles. . . .

Other canons forbid the sale of forbidden books expressly mentioned in the *Index of Forbidden Books*. The present legislation includes all kinds of publications: books, booklets, pamphlets, periodicals, newspapers and the like.

The term "obscene" covers those matters whether real or imaginative which arouse the lower passions. However, a publication is not to be judged obscene simply if it offends against a local convention of propriety.

For the book to come under the present law, the obscenity must be explicit. It must be made directly and be prominent. The latter term is currently defined as dominating in a large section of the text, for example, a whole chapter. . . .

Not all books which may be construed as obscene are banned by the canon. Medical, legal, and scientific works dealing with these subjects, the purpose of which is to present to students in the professions a true understanding of social or medical problems, are permitted. It is important that these publications do not fall into the hands of those whose minds are not prepared for mature reading.

There is no explicit canon concerning librarians. However, a librarian, working in a reference or public library, is acting primarily not as an individual but as an agent of the institution that employs him. As such he can neither exploit his position for religious propaganda nor impose Catholic restrictions upon non-Catholic readers. In any case of serious doubt, his spiritual director will instruct him whether to conform to his secular duties or resign his position. In the case of a Catholic library, of course, the situation is entirely different and the canonical prescriptions must be explicitly observed. . . .

The Catholic Church has always been concerned about books injurious to faith. That her position is still firm and unyielding is indicated in this rule that forbids "books of any writers defending or championing heresy or schism, or attempting in any way to undermine the foundations of religion." . . .

Heresy consists in a denial of the truths that have been defined and proposed by the Church as divinely revealed doctrines. Any baptized person of the Catholic faith who denies or doubts any of these truths is known as a heretic.

Schism is the refusal of a baptized Catholic to recognize the religious authority of the pope or to maintain communion with members of the Church. . . .

As a general class, "books which avowedly attack religion and good morals," are condemned.

The term "religion" is not here restricted to the Catholic faith, but the condemnation includes all books which openly attack divine worship in general.

"Good morals" applies to ethics and all that pertains to right living. Books that attack the natural law are automatically forbidden. Also condemned are those books opposing any of the commandments, and those defending divorce, suicide, abortion, or contraception. Immoral writings come under this class if their main purpose is to attack and destroy the laws of good morals. . . .

The Catholic Church legislates to control error which corrupts the faith. The definition condemns "books of any non-Catholic writer which professedly treat of religion, unless it is certain that they contain nothing contrary to the Catholic religion." . . .

The third and final general class of forbidden writings may be grouped under morals.

Superstitious Books. St. Thomas Aquinas defines superstition as "a vice opposed to religion by way of excess, because it offers divine worship to beings other than God." The Church opposes superstition whenever and wherever practiced. . . .

In all these general rules, it is well to distinguish the matter of which the book treats from the manner in which it is treated. A book, in order to be classed within this group, must fulfill certain conditions: The book must not only treat of one of the above-mentioned subjects, but it must also (1) endeavor to prove it to be lawful in the sense and to the extent that it is condemned by the Church; (2) present the subject in such a manner as to attempt to influence the reader. . . .

The entire legislation of the Church against writings regarded as dangerous to faith and morals is commonly referred to as the *Index.* This leads some to the false notion that the literary policy of the Church is governed solely by a heterogeneous catalogue of banned books and authors, known as the *Index of Forbidden Books.* It is likewise erroneously assumed that the *Index* is intended to be a complete list of all heretical and immoral literature.

The *Index of Forbidden Books* is not and was never designed to be a complete catalogue of forbidden literature. The *Index* is merely a list of condemned books by the Holy See in response to specific requests submitted by persons throughout the world. . . . The majority of cases referred to the Congregation of the Holy Office deal with theological matters or doctrines that have actually become issues in a particular locality, and which in the opinion of the local bishop require official condemnation. Canon 1399 sets forth the general classifications of books that are restricted even though they may never appear in the pages of the *Index*. The catalogue of condemned authors and titles is but a supplement to the general classes mentioned in Canon 1399. . . .

Permission may be obtained by any Catholic to peruse forbidden books when there is a justifiable reason. Benedict XIV draws particular attention to the obligations of Catholic scientists to read forbidden scientific writings:

So valuable for the influence of people is the example of the men of science, that it is not too much to say that even in the work of scientific investigation it is their duty . . . to secure a dispensation for the reading of prohibited works or doubtful books.

Presumptive Permission. It may happen that a scholar or student suddenly finds it necessary to read a work explicitly condemned or falling into one of the general classes of forbidden writings in connection with his duties and cannot possibly obtain the required permission in time. These emergency cases do arise. In such cases the individual may reasonably presume permission to read the particular book. For example, a judge may be called upon to evaluate an immoral book in a secular court. A professor, a Catholic librarian in a public library, a lecturer, a writer, a priest, or a newspaper editor may be called upon to present a prompt explanation of the Catholic position.

A very special form of this problem constantly faces Catholic librarians and teachers. The number of books examined by Church authorities is very small. Of the annual production of books in the United States, which during the past few years averaged eleven thousand volumes, not a single condemnation was pronounced by the Congregation of the Holy Office. Yet obviously many of them must violate many principles of Catholicism.

Immorality, profane love, pseudo philosophy as well as pseudo theology have become so common especially in recent times that the public taste is dulled and secular reviewers may by no means be relied upon to discriminate on moral issues.

The obligation of their office as librarians or as teachers of literature obliges Catholics in these positions to read and evaluate works of doubtful character which will never be mentioned by any official Catholic media. An exceptionally healthy mindedness is needed here, since excessive scruples will undo all good which might be hoped for. Many schools and libraries will have no other censor than the teacher or librarian. From this obligation arises an implied permission to read doubtful books and publications under this canon, but individuals, finding themselves in this situation, must secure permission to read books of this nature. This special permission usually is granted for three-year periods and may be renewed.

There is no justification or necessity for any reading that may be an impulse to serious sin. But here the axiom holds true that "what is one man's meat may be another man's poison." It depends upon the character and disposition of each individual. If a reader knows from experience that a certain type of reading will cause certain doubts about his faith which he is unable to resolve, he must not read the books even though special permission has been granted.

MORAL CENSORSHIP

EDITOR'S INTRODUCTION

Starting off with an article by a freelance writer on the wide newsstand display of questionable books and magazines, this section contains arguments for and against "controls" on moral grounds, presented by representatives of religious groups, public authorities and persons associated with the publishing business.

A leader of the National Council of Catholic Men and a Catholic editor offer views that are challenged by the director of the American Civil Liberties Union and the chairman of the Reprinters' (of paper-books) Committee. Some of this material is drawn from the report of the House of Representatives Select Committee on the Study of Current Pornographic Materials, commonly called the Gathings Committee. The principal recommendations of that committee are quoted.

A publisher pleads that censorship be left to the public taste. A liberal Catholic editor and a publisher of paper-bound books discuss the merits and defects of these volumes. A book and magazine distributor warns that public pressures may compel dealers to refuse to handle some of these publications. An editor urges that booksellers give more heed to the wants of their customers.

Two police officials tell how they enforce censorship ordinances. A judge's opinion, quoted here, restrains one of these police officials.

Finally, a Protestant church publication points to the dangers in the rapid spread of "vigilante" censorship.

SMUT ON OUR NEWSSTANDS [1]

All in all, filth adds up to a profitable business. . . . Twilight publishers issue about one third of the 1200 magazine titles that

---

[1] From an article by J. Alvin Kugelmass, freelance writer, formerly of editorial staff of *Christian Herald*. *Christian Herald*. p21-2+. May 1952. Reprinted by permission.

may be found on newsstands, and are powerful, even cocky. But they can't stand up against an alerted citizenry!

Your town can do a housecleaning job on its magazine stands—with or without police backing. There is not a state in the land which does not have one or more statutes under which obscenity may be seized and destroyed. Yet officials are reluctant to take steps. They say they are fearful of treading across the borderline into censorship! . . .

It requires no great amount of literary acumen or puritanism to label each and every one of these magazines as obscene. The phrase "freedom of the press" has frightened people into holding their tongues in defiance of their indignation and innate good sense. No less a critic than John Mason Brown had no hesitancy in calling these publications "the lowest, most despicable, most harmful and unethical form of trash." . . .

Not only are too many of us giving aid and assistance to the smut peddlers by our silence, but ironically we are all, as taxpayers, underwriting them financially! Under an Act of Congress dated March 3, 1879 (and brought up to date February 2, 1928), subparagraph 4, section 412, *Postal Laws & Regulations*, states that any publication devised to further "education" in the United States may enjoy a second-class mailing permit. About 90 per cent of the shady publishers avail themselves of this permit. They get a less-than-cost rate in mailing copies in bulk to distribution points across the country. . . . [Yet] the loss to the Post Office last year in handling second-class mail came to $250 million. These publishers are happy about the permit for two reasons: first, their profits are far greater because the taxpayer helps to foot their postage bill; second, they can point to the permit, lift their eyes piously and exclaim, "We are called educational by the Government itself!"

Why doesn't the Post Office Department cancel the permits of the filth purveyors? Because the postal authorities, too, have been scared by the censorship bugaboo. This despite the fact numerous Federal laws actually forbid the mailing of obscene literature. . . .

Sometimes when a particularly bestial crime or orgiastic cellar club of teen-agers is traced back to provocative magazines, a state or city will rush through a harsh and oppressive censorship law which does no one any good and indeed affects the orderly and free distribution of the reputable or "class" magazines. The twilight boys then sit back while class publishers in effect fight in their defense! No new laws are needed. There are plenty of laws on the books. All we need to do is enforce them.

A good example of laxity was recently brought to light in Newark, New Jersey. Clergy and citizenry, aroused over crimes and sex parties which were linked to obscene magazines, called for action. The chief law-enforcement officer of Newark threatened news dealers by saying, "I am prepared to enforce the law." (One cannot understand why he had not been doing so and why it was necessary to threaten. For a Newark ordinance passed in 1936 provided for fines up to $200, plus ninety days in jail, for the sale of literature whose legal description neatly matched fact-detective, girlie and nudist publications.) Where the police failed to act, the Parent-Teachers Association, church groups, clergymen and responsible businessmen were alerted. Within twenty-four hours after the drive began, the stands were cleared of smut. What the volunteer workers did was to travel about town, especially to those stands near schools, and talk with the proprietors. The news dealers were only too happy to comply.

Many a newsstand man is repelled by the wares he sells. But he is forced to carry trash if he wants to get class. In Phoenix, Arizona, Covina, California, and New Britain, Connecticut, to cite a few, dealers who refused to carry filth they themselves would be ashamed of reading, found themselves starved out, cut off from all other publications. One owner of several drug stores in California appealed to the public to help him. He took large advertisements in the local newspapers revealing the pressure put upon him by distributors when he refused to accept obscene magazines. The public rallied and he won the American right to select his merchandise.

On the community level, without the need of new laws, the policeman's stick or hysterical censorship—church groups, the P.T.A. and clergymen, banding together, have found the task of cleanup a fairly easy one.

In Lynn, Masachussetts, such a coalition, headed by the P.T.A., which has been in the forefront of a nation-wide drive to deodorize the newsstands, was immediately effective. News dealers were given a list of obviously objectionable magazines and were warned that their stands would be boycotted if they carried them. The list in Lynn is revised now and then and the police are furnished with revised lists.

Similar drives, undertaken in Bayonne, New Jersey, Beatrice, Nebraska, Los Angeles, San Diego and New Orleans, have been amazingly successful. The news dealer, when assured of community sentiment, pressures the distributor who then informs the publisher—and it's either clean up or close up. No seller can live without buyers.

Your town doesn't have to take it lying down. Your town can fight back, and will fight when it knows it is struggling for its moral life. But a cleanup won't begin by itself. Somebody has to start. Here's what to do:

1. If you live in a small community, take a look at the newsstand yourself—not as a censor, but as a citizen sufficiently astute to know the difference between black and white. Talk to the dealer. See how he feels about the problem. Perhaps he has never thought about it at all, or realized that he was making an outstanding contribution to delinquency. With your personal backing he may be able to clean up immediately.

2. If you live in a larger community (say, over a thousand population), or if the dealer gives you an indignant brush-off, haul up your big guns. Organize a flying unit of the P.T.A. This special committee can obtain advice on the best way of proceeding from the national P.T.A. . . .

3. Combine the P.T.A. unit with a committee composed of clergymen of all faiths. If possible, get an English teacher or two to sit in on the group in an advisory capacity.

4. Bitter but necessary dose: purchase as many of the lurid magazines as are displayed on the newsstands. They can be quickly recognized. The expenditure by your cleanup committee of ten to twenty dollars is justified. Except for a further outlay of energy, this will be the only cost. Then, as a committee, hold your nose—and read!

5. Get up a list of the magazines you would be ashamed of reading and which you would not want your children to read. Again, this is easier than one might suppose. Where there is a reasonable doubt, hold your fire; there are too many magazines that are overboard in filth to get into an argument about those that are only teetering on the edge. If you have no criterion, examine the advertising. If a magazine is filthy and deliberately designed so, it will scream filth at you.

6. Tour the community and talk with every drug store and stationery store owner and every newsstand dealer. If this is your first round, you will likely find him cooperative. He too lives in the community, probably has a family, and as a rule is tired of peddling filth. If this is your second visit, he knows now that you mean business. Don't order him to discontinue using these publications. Merely suggest it by giving him the list. He will immediately contact his distributor.

7. To help the retailer, go to see the distributor. If he behaves unpleasantly, show him a copy of the state or local laws on obscenity. If he pleads that he will be ruined financially, don't believe him. He can make a handsome income from the eight hundred or so good titles.

8. If distributor and newsdealers balk, go to the city editor of your local newspaper. Enlist his aid in doing a series of articles. When the stories run, drop in on the district attorney or chief of police.

9. Register a complaint with your local postmaster—each and every time a shipment of objectionable magazines comes into your town through the mails. Write your congressman and senators, naming offensive publications.

A CATHOLIC SUGGESTS CONTROLS [2]

The program of action in the field of objectionable literature carried out by the National Council of Catholic Men and other

[2] From testimony by the Reverend Thomas J. Fitzgerald, representative of the National Council of Catholic Men, Chicago, December 2, 1952. In Report of the House of Representatives Select Committee on Current Pornographic Materials. 82d Congress, 2d session. Superintendent of Documents, Washington 25, D.C. 1952. p47.

Catholic organizations throughout the country is based on a code against which magazines, pocket-size books, and comics are judged.

Publications are listed as objectionable which (1) Glorify or condone reprehensible characters or reprehensible acts; (2) Contain material offensively "sexy"; (3) Feature illicit love; (4) Carry illustrations indecent or suggestive, or (5) Advertise wares for the prurient-minded.

The National Organization for Decent Literature publishes each month, as a guide to individuals and groups who desire to take steps to minimize or eliminate the damage caused by objectionable literature, a list of objectionable magazines, pocket-size books, and comics.

No one can accurately estimate the incalculable harm that is being done to American society by the deliberate publication, widespread distribution, and open sale in food markets, drug stores, newsstands, and many other retail outlets of literature that appeals to the lowest instincts of man.

I should like to limit my formal testimony before this committee to a few suggestions that might help to stop the flood of objectionable comics, magazines, and pocket-size books. They are:

1. The most logical means to control the problem would be for industry itself to establish a code with the cooperation of religious, civic, and educational leaders. This code would act as a guide to an industry reviewing board similar to that used by the motion picture and television industries.

2. We also recommend that the committee take steps to create an informed and alert public opinion among all civic-minded groups. It is suggested that the national officers of such organizations as the National Council of Catholic Men and the National Council of Catholic Women, the Parent-Teacher Associations, the Girl Scouts and Boy Scouts, the Kiwanis, the Rotary, the Lions, the General Federation of Women's Clubs, etc., be invited by the committee to view the publications that have been submitted and their cooperation asked at the local level to make sure these types of publications are not available to our youth. . . .

It would be most unfortunate indeed if this honest inquiry into such a serious matter were to be distorted by press, radio, or television into an attack on freedom of the press. The question here is not one of freedom but one of license.

I think it was Justice Oliver Wendell Holmes who made the famous statement that freedom of speech does not entitle a person to shout "fire" in a crowded theater.

I firmly believe that the majority of the people in the industry feel very strongly about this particular subject, as we do. They feel that the industry is getting a bad name as a result of the work of a few in the industry, and just as the movie industry, the television industry, as a result of the same type of evil, you might call it, creeping into the industry, did something about it, I feel that if these men were approached, and a reviewing board was suggested to them, and they were to have a series of meetings about this particular subject, that they would work it out.

After all, you have got a czar in baseball; you have got a czar in pro football, just to keep those two sports from having any reflection on their integrity; and why shouldn't you have some sort of a reviewing board similarly in this particular field that would protect the honest publisher?

THE "RIGHT TO OBJECT" [3]

A group of Brooklyn citizens, members of the Holy Name Society of Our Lady Help of Christians parish, decided recently that they would do something about objectionable literature displayed in candy and news stores. In pairs they visited sixteen stores and, reminding the owners that narcotics and liquor could not be sold to children, asked them not to sell "poison for the minds" of the youngsters. All the owners agreed to cooperate, although two were a little rebellious.

Immediately the New York *Post* raised the cry of "censorship" in an indignant editorial (February 22, 1953).

[3] From "The 'Right to Object' Against Smut," editorial. *America.* 86:611. March 7, 1953; and "Fight on Banning Objectionable Books," editorial. 88:668. March 21, 1953. Reprinted by permission.

The *Post* missed the point. There was no censorship involved. What the citizens did was simply to exercise their constitutional right—and their parental duty—of asking dealers not to sell the youngsters matter they did not want their children to read. It is true that if the stores had not cooperated they would likely have lost considerable patronage. But is it not within the citizens' right to patronize only those stores whose wares they conceive not to be a moral danger to children? . . .

They are exercising their right to object—even to object in organized fashion. If their objections are yielded to, it will, of course, follow that others who may not agree with those objections will not be able to pick up such reading matter indiscriminately at the corner store. Their freedom will be, to that extent, limited. But to claim that the objectors have thereby "taken the law into their own hands" is to overlook such a valid parallel as the picket-line—a venerable American example of the right to object.

LIMITS OF THE RIGHT TO OBJECT [4]

The American Civil Liberties Union defends, as being within both the letter and the spirit of the Constitution, any simple expression by any individual or group of disapproval of any book (or film, play, periodical, radio program, etc.) or any attempt simply to dissuade others from buying it.

The ACLU recognizes, as far as legal right is concerned, the use of such orderly and lawful means as peaceful and unobstructive picketing and the organization of a specific and primary boycott, even when they imply some degree of coercion. . . .

The Union recognizes that the problem of "pressure-group censorship" is full of differences in degree, and that it is hard to draw lines which represent the best possible combination of the freedom of expression and the freedom to see what is offered on the one hand, and the freedom to protest effectively, on the other hand.

[4] From "ACLU Policy Statement on Pressure-Group Censorship," pamphlet. American Civil Liberties Union. 170 Fifth Avenue. New York. 1952. p2. Reprinted by permission.

But it believes that intimidation and reprisal have no place in the field of ideas.

The ever-increasing attempts of private pressure-groups to bring about the censorship or suppression of motion pictures, etc., which they disapprove—either through public officials or directly—dangerously undermine one of the foundation stones of American democracy, the freedom of expression. (This is especially true in the case of such operations as are secretly financed or conducted.)

The Union therefore pledges itself to intensify its efforts to investigate and combat this dangerous tendency, by all appropriate methods.

It urges those responsible for the publication or production, the distribution or circulation or exhibition, of newspapers, periodicals or books, of radio or television programs, of plays, motion pictures or other theatrical entertainments, to stand firmly against this threat to the freedom of their industries and the freedom of the people as a whole.

In accordance with its long-established policy, the ACLU will refrain from expressing disapproval of the contents of any book, etc., unless in the opinion of the Board extraordinary circumstances necessitate such expression.

THE RISKS OF FREE SPEECH [5]

The American Civil Liberties Union is the only nation-wide nonpartisan organization whose sole function is to defend the guarantees of the Bill of Rights of the United States Constitution for everybody. One of these guarantees, protected by the First Amendment to our Constitution, is freedom of speech and a free press. . . . Freedom of speech and press, which is the major distinguishing factor between our way of life . . . [and] communism and other forms of totalitarianism, means freedom from censorship. We appear here today to urge that this com-

[5] From testimony by Patrick Murphy Malin, Executive Director, American Civil Liberties Union, before the House of Representatives Select Committee on Current Pornographic Materials, December 5, 1952. Mimeographed. American Civil Liberties Union. 170 Fifth Avenue. New York. 1952. p 1-6. Reprinted by permission.

mittee recommend for legislation nothing that can interfere with
that freedom, and that it take steps by enactment of new legislation and amendment of existing legislation to alleviate certain
restrictions on freedom of the press.

We recognize that under the existing interpretation of the
Constitution, obscene material does not have the protection of
the First Amendment. But we are concerned that the laws of
obscenity and criminal libel may be used to improperly punish
publication of material which is properly within the protection
of the First Amendment. We do not believe that there is any
constitutional right to circulate "dirt for dirt's sake," and we
have indeed refrained from intervening in many cases which we
do not feel involve civil liberties. . . . Our sole criterion is
this: that subject to the right of the state to punish criminally
the dissemination of obscene material, no American is competent
to tell any other American what he may read. It is not only
the freedom of the publisher that is at stake. It is also the
freedom of 160 million Americans whose Constitution guarantees
them that no governmental official may tell them what they may
or may not read.

The two major problems with which this committee is concerned are (1) the dissemination of obscene material and (2)
of material dealing excessively with crime.

Each of the forty-eight states has laws against the dissemination of obscene material. Those laws are more than adequate
to deal with the problem. While the cry of states' rights is
rarely heard in this context, we suggest that because of different
standards in different communities, local criminal prosecution for
obscenity is the best way to handle this problem. . . .

The second major problem with which this committee is
concerned is allegedly from material "placing improper emphasis
on crime, violence and corruption." Assuming for the purposes
of argument that legislators or anyone else knows what emphasis
on crime is proper and what emphasis is improper, there are
serious constitutional objections that arise.

The only possible way of avoiding the Scylla of vagueness in
dealing with such material is by setting up a licensing system.
But such a precensorship of material clearly runs afoul of the

Charybdis of the First Amendment which unequivocally prohibits the licensing of books.

We are disturbed by newspaper reports that suggestions have been made to this committee that it endorse the formation of volunteer citizens groups in each state and in local communities to serve as "watch-dog committees" and attempt to influence book dealers into refusing to handle books the committees consider improper. We vigorously oppose this recommendation, because it constitutes another form of censorship. In effect, it would set up self-appointed vigilantes proceeding without standards and responsible to no authorized body. It would give vast power—without responsibility—to certain individuals over other individuals. We, of course, recognize that individuals do have the right to protest as an exercise of their right of free speech, but when the purpose of such speech is suppression, then we must register our objections. . . .

Another suggestion is that of a publishers' code of censorship. . . . While a code of good taste by and of itself is certainly appropriate—we all want good and better taste in our literature—we oppose a code which, in effect, would close the avenues of free expression to writers. To be more specific: while we would not object to a publisher's association giving its seal or stamp of approval to literature it feels meets the standard of good taste, we would object to any code which prohibited writers from writing what they wanted, merely because the publishers would object to it, and when their writings violated no law. . . .

Just as laws against obscenity which protect adults also protect children, so any laws which would censor comic books or pocket books for children must also censor the same reading material for adults. It would be a sad day if no adult could read material unless it has been screened first for children.

All that I have said does not mean that action cannot be taken to curb the abuses that arise in this field. Such action is already taking place in American homes, schools, the churches and synagogues—all mustered to do battle with any evil tendencies, if such there be, that crime books may bring out. Are we to say that these forces are powerless? Are we to say that all children and all adults must be insulated from all temptation?

How are [we] ever to learn to meet temptation if we do not have an opportunity to learn to meet *with* it first? Somehow, gentlemen, everyone feels that some type of literature does harm to somebody else, not to him. And yet, no one can find the particular people that the literature does do harm to.

There may be, in the absence of censorship, some risk that some persons along the line may possibly get hurt. But our life is founded upon risk. There is risk—and indeed certainty—that every day many people will be killed by automobiles, and yet we leave automobiles on our streets. I suggest to you that the institution of free speech is surely just as vital to our society as the automobile. Risk there is in all life, and we must take this risk on the side of freedom. That is the glory of our way of life. Censorship is abhorrent to Americanism. We urge this committee therefore to take action to protect freedom of the press against the excesses we have mentioned before and to help to free completely an already partly encumbered press.

GATHINGS COMMITTEE PROPOSALS [6]

The recommendations of the committee fall into two general categories: (1) Those steps which should be taken in order to control, more effectively, the distribution of obscene materials generally, (2) those steps which should be taken with respect to objectionable books, magazines, and comics.

Recommendation 1. Enactment of legislation . . . rendering it a Federal offense to knowingly transport in interstate or foreign commerce for sale or distribution certain specified articles and matters, including books and pamphlets of an obscene, lewd, lascivious, or filthy character.

At present, the interstate transportation of such matter is proscribed only to the extent that it is deposited with an express company or other common carrier for carriage in interstate commerce. . . . There is no Federal law prohibiting the transportation of obscene materials in interstate commerce by private carrier. Information supplied by the Department of Justice and

[6] From Report of the House of Representatives Select Committee on Current Pornographic Materials. 82d Congress, 2d session. Superintendent of Documents, Washington 25, D.C. 1952. p 116-20.

local enforcement officers indicates that the purveyors of pornographic materials are fully aware of this weakness in the law, and transport such materials by automobile, or on their persons, across state lines, realizing that in so doing they are completely immune to Federal prosecution.

Recommendation 2. Enactment of legislation authorizing (1) the Postmaster General to impound mail *pendende lite* [pending trial] which is addressed to a person or concern which is obtaining or attempting to obtain remittances of money through the mails in exchange for any obscene, lewd, lascivious, indecent, filthy or vile article, matter, thing, device, or substance, and (2) exemption of the Post Office Department from the provisions of the Administrative Procedure Act.

Under the law, at the present time, the Postmaster General is authorized to order returned to the sender all mail addressed to any person or concern obtaining or attempting to obtain remittances of money through the mails by means of false or fraudulent pretenses, representations, and promises; obtaining or attempting to obtain remittances of money through the mails in exchange for any obscene, lewd, lascivious, indecent, filthy or vile article, matter, thing, device or substance; is engaged in conducting through the mails any lottery or drawing; or in the conduct of an unlawful business is using and is requested to be addressed by a fictitious, false, or assumed name, title or address. . . .

Two courses of action are available to the Postmaster General in preventing the use of mails for the dissemination of obscene materials:

1. Section 1461 of title 18, United States Code, reads in part as follows:

Every obscene, lewd, lascivious, or filthy book, pamphlet, picture, paper, letter, writing, print, or other publication of an indecent character . . . is declared to be nonmailable matter and shall not be conveyed in the mails or delivered from any post office or by any letter carrier.

Postmasters, in preparing mails for dispatch, may inspect all mail which is not under first-class cover. . . . If the postmaster is in doubt concerning the mailability of the article, he withdraws it from the mail and submits it to the Solicitor's Office of the Post Office Department for an opinion as to its mailability.

Should the Solicitor believe that the material is in fact obscene and, therefore, in violation of section 1461 of title 18, United States Code, he advises the postmaster that he has concluded that the material is nonmailable. The postmaster is further advised to notify the person who deposited the material in the mails that within a stipulated period of time he may appear before the Solicitor and present such views as he might desire in connection with the proposed ruling. If, after hearing the mailer, the Solicitor is still of the opinion that the matter is still nonmailable, he instructs the postmaster at the point of mailing to treat the matter as nonmailable. It should be emphasized that this action is available only where the mailing is other than first class. As a result, the great bulk of obscene or border-line materials are, if the mails are used at all, sent first class, thus denying the postmaster the opportunity to preliminarily inspect the material prior to dispatch.

2. "Unlawful" business orders: "Unlawful" orders may be issued by the Postmaster General . . . when he is satisfied that any person or concern is receiving remittances of money through the mails in exchange for obscene, lewd, lascivious, or indecent materials. The issuance of such an order by the Postmaster [General] serves as an instruction to the postmaster to return to senders any mail addressed to the charged person or concern marked "unlawful." It also prohibits the negotiation of any money order made to the order of the person or concern conducting the unlawful business. . . . It should also be noted that the "unlawful" order does not forbid the person or concern conducting the unlawful business from posting outgoing mail which, of course, could include more obscene materials. The fundamental purpose of the "unlawful" order is the cutting off of the fruits of the crime.

In either instance, the person or concern affected by the issuance of an "unlawful" order or by the Solicitor's ruling with respect to the mailability of a particular item may, of course, seek relief in the district courts of the United States. . . .

It has been shown that many enterprises involving the sale of obscene materials are so planned and operated that they inflict swift and irreparable injury to the public in such a comparatively short time that they would be practically immune to any effective interference by the issuance of an "unlawful" order. . . . In one recent case, a person charged with selling obscene pictures advertised to his customers that the Post Office Department was accusing him of selling indecent materials. He actually employed the terminology of the statute—namely "lewd, lascivious, indecent, and obscene"—as descriptive advertising adjectives, and coupled this with an urgent appeal for orders prior to the date when he calculated that he could no longer do business through the mails.

By the enactment of legislation authorizing the Postmaster General to impound mail addressed to a concern which he has reason to believe is disseminating obscene materials, and against whom he has filed a complaint for the purpose of obtaining the issuance of an "unlawful" order, pending the outcome of the proceeding and the exemption of the Post Office Department from the requirements of the Administrative Procedure Act, this type of operation would be substantially curtailed. . . .

Fortunately, there has been no clear decision by the courts that the determination by the Solicitor of the Post Office Department with respect to the "mailability" of a particular material must be reached only after the requirements of the Administrative Procedure Act have been observed. Should such a requirement be imposed on the Post Office Department, an almost insurmountable barrier would be placed in the way of the effective policing of the mails insofar as obscene materials are concerned. For example, in the fiscal year 1952, 1,700 rulings were made by the Solicitor with respect to obscene materials. The impracticability of holding 1,700 hearings on matters of this kind in accordance with the detailed procedural requirements of the Administrative Procedure Act is apparent.

Recommendation 3. That the publishing industry recognize the growing public opposition to that proportion of its output which may be classified as "borderline" or "objectionable," and take the steps necessary to its elimination on its own initiative, rather than to allow this opposition to increase to the point where the public will demand governmental action.

TRUST THE PEOPLE'S JUDGMENT [7]

Recently, while standing by the desk of Representative E. S. Gathings (Democrat, Arkansas) in the House Office Building, Washington, we found it difficult to avoid being startled by a sprawling mass of lurid magazines and books. The sordid covers and contents, dedicated to violence, raw sex, and crime created their own shock of surprise that such publications are sold openly on United States newsstands.

As chairman of a special committee recently created by Congress, Representative Gathings reported he was explicitly empowered to investigate (1) "the extent to which current literature—books, magazines and comic books—containing immoral, obscene, or otherwise offensive matter, or placing improper emphasis on crime, violence, and corruption are being made available to the people of the United States through the United States mails and otherwise," and (2) "to determine the adequacy of existing laws to prevent the publication and distribution of books containing immoral, offensive, and otherwise undesirable matter." . . .

Observing Representative Gathings's earnest approach to his inquiry, it was difficult not to agree quickly and completely with him. . . .

Still underneath the valid provocation, the obvious abuse, there was a nagging of doubt. An important principle of American freedom possibly was being obscured because of the sordidness of the exhibits cluttering Representative Gathings's desk.

Perhaps the Washington *Post* put its finger on the heart of the matter when the Gathings resolution on books was originally being considered in the House. A *Post* editorial commented:

Here is an indubitably pious resolution embracing dangerously vague concepts. Who can say what constitutes "offensive matter" or precisely what degree of emphasis on crime, violence, and corruption is "improper"? This investigation would be a threat to every publisher. It would amount, in effect, to a form of intimidation. Defective and some-

[7] From "The Censors and the Public," by W. D. Patterson, associate publisher, *Saturday Review*. *Saturday Review*. 35:22-3. September 6, 1952. Reprinted by permission.

times sordid as the products of the American printing presses may be, it is best to leave these products to the judgment of the public. There is not such a thing as good censorship. . . .

The fact that the Gathings committee would lead us down a dangerous road, however, should not allow us to minimize the necessity of the most searching consideration by responsible executives in publishing . . . of their own responsibility for the products they offer the public. Their hands are not blameless. The answer to censorship in a democracy is the progressive education of the public taste to reject the bad and demand the good, without recourse to official censors or to the extremism of many private pressure groups.

Furthermore, it should be particularly noted that what has been under discussion here is the flagrant excesses among publications, books and radio-TV rather than the fine thought, great literature, wholesome adventure, and good music that they are bringing the public in ever larger measure. The best of the pocket-book publishers, for example are reprinting for an appreciative mass audience more and more the best of contemporary and traditional literature.

To trust the judgment of the people—in cultural as in political matters—in a time of stress and suspicion is the real test of a democracy.

ART AND PRUDENCE [8]

The New American Library of World Literature, publishers of the paper-bound Signet and Mentor books, has made some outstanding contributions to the level of popular American culture. Among its titles have been works of great literary and intellectual distinction, made easily available, for the first time, to a general audience in the United States. And not the least of its achievements has been the publication of *New World Writing*, a popular-priced anthology of serious (and sometimes original) creative and critical work.

[8] From "Sex and Censorship," editorial. *Commonweal.* 53:193-4. May 29, 1953. Reprinted by permission.

The third number of this anthology has recently appeared. Its lead article, an essay on "Sex and Censorship in Contemporary Society," by Margaret Mead, has a special interest. The problem it deals with has been a matter of national controversies recently, and in these controversies the New American Library itself has played a central, consistently partisan, role. Many of its own titles have been attacked as "immoral," and some of them have been removed from distribution and sale in local communities.

Debate on the issues involved has been hot. The apparently conflicting claims of Art and Prudence have been vigorously made, and some wise things have been said, by both sides. But both sides have said some rather foolish things too, and in the process the real issue has frequently been obscured. An attempt to restate it has been increasingly needed.

Dr. Mead's essay meets this need with great success. The real issue, as she sees it, is the distinction between what is genuinely pornographic and what, for one reason or another, might seem to be. Against the genuinely pornographic the community must, of course, protect itself—through legislation, if necessary. But, she insists,

> Legislative decrees are only half the answer—it is also important that the guns of those who embody organized values, those who care about religion, those who care about literature and art—should be trained against labeling anything pornographic which is not pornographic.
> Actually [Dr. Mead concludes], it is as important at present to legislate against false labeling as against the content of a particular book. Every time a publisher puts a cover on a twenty-five-cent edition of a serious and important book promising illicit delights to the prurient, the issue between pornography on the one hand and literature, art, science and ethics on the other is obscured. . . . If every publisher who issued a serious work in a pornographic wrapper was subject to indictment similar —although paradoxically in reverse—to prosecution under the Pure Food and Drug Act, we might begin to steer our way through this maze in which we find ourselves.

Precisely. During the past year the maze has grown thicker. Numerous groups from the congressional Gathings Committee to the local "Decent Literature" leagues, have attacked the sale of "immoral" books which were high among the literary and intellectual classics of our century.

But, in spite of the bitter charges, it has seemed doubtful that the various "Decent Literature" groups are really interested in destroying freedom of mind or that the publishers actually intend to corrupt the morals of the nation. It has seemed, rather, that in most instances the former have looked only at the often lurid covers, and the latter only at what was inside. For many of the books attacked are not, in any legitimate sense of the word, "pornographic"—but many of them have been made to appear so by the publishers themselves.

The need for distinguishing here is great and the obligation to do so lies heavy on both sides. Margaret Mead's essay is a valuable contribution to this end. One hopes that its lesson will be learned by some who have offended gravely in this question—including a certain publisher who has, in other ways, "made some outstanding contributions to the level of popular American culture."

A PUBLISHER'S REPLY [9]

I and my fellow publishers of inexpensive editions, reprint and original, are now fighting in many American communities for the right to sell books which have been arbitrarily banned on the charge of alleged obscenity. I am not speaking of smutty books, produced to exploit dirt for dirt's sake, which rightly should be driven out of circulation. That can easily be done under existing laws. I am speaking of books by William Faulkner, John Steinbeck, James T. Farrell, Somerset Maugham, Erskine Caldwell, Ernest Hemingway and scores of distinguished modern authors. I am also speaking of books of secondary literary importance which by no stretch of the imagination can be legally found pornographic. These bans usually apply to books deemed "objectionable" by the Chicago Archdiocese Council of Catholic Women—a list of which is publicized throughout the country—and enforced by police officials or by organized boycotts.

[9] From "The Attack on Books: a Publisher's Analysis," address by Victor Weybright, chairman and editor, New American Library of World Literature, Inc., and chairman, Reprinters' Committee, American Book Publishers Council, before the Conference on College Composition, Chicago, March 14, 1953. *Publishers' Weekly.* 163:1511-13. April 4, 1953. Reprinted by permission.

Far from defending pornography, or advocating the circulation of obscene books, I strongly urge the enforcement of existing laws against obscenity, sedition or libel. Most of the states and many cities have on their books stringent statutes directed at printed matter which is obscene. The Federal laws expressly prohibit interstate movement of books which are obscene or filthy, and in fact the American Book Publishers Council endorsed a bill just passed which extended this prohibition to private conveyances as well as common carriers. The standards are definite and likewise the legal interpretations of them. The legal principle of the law of censorship established in Federal and state courts is that the question of obscenity must be determined by an appraisal of the predominant effect of a book read as a whole. . . .

I do not quarrel with the right of any group, political or sectarian, to recommend to its own members that they abstain from the reading of books which such a group may disapprove. I do not quarrel either with the right or duty of parents to exercise control upon the reading matter they consider suitable or unsuitable for their children. The activities of such groups become vicious, however, when they seek to impose upon members of the general public, private standards of their own which differ from the standards established and enforced by law.

In today's mood of orthodoxy any noncomformist is suspect. Books, as the most important vehicles for boldness of thought and human imagination, are, therefore, a natural target for anti-intellectual minorities who fear the free human mind and the discipline of the free human conscience. . . .

The censors, and especially the precensors seem totally to lack faith in the role of parents, the school and of the church; they would deny to adults what may possibly be read by the young. The essential point of this matter is that most books are not basically designed for children or aimed at the juvenile. Generally speaking our market [for paper-bound] reprints except for specialized efforts in the educational or juvenile field, is a popular adult market—the same market served by the standard trade publisher, the corner book store, the public library, the magazines and daily and weekly newspapers. I believe, along with many of our educators and some of our jurists, that a child old enough to understand or to be interested in these books—or the newspapers, for that matter—cannot be harmed by them. Some of them deal with fundamentally adult subjects and may, perhaps, have an impact on a younger reader which would be better postponed till he has more experience and understanding. But certainly the whole adult reading public should not be denied the enlightenment and understanding to be derived from the reading of good literature to prevent an occasional child from reading a book or a newspaper designed primarily for adult consumption. The responsibility for what children read resides in the home, the school and the church.

This view was most effectively stated by Judge Curtis G. Bok, March 18, 1949, in his Pennsylvania decision with reference to a group of books which he cleared of the charge of obscenity. Judge Bok said:

It will be asked whether one would care to have one's young daughter read these books. I suppose that by the time she is old enough to wish to read them she will have learned the biologic facts of life and the words that go with them. There is something seriously wrong at home if those facts have not been met and faced and sorted by then; it is not children so much as parents that should receive our concern about this. I should prefer that my own three daughters meet the facts of life and the literature of the world in my library than behind a neighbor's barn, for I can face the adversary there directly. If the young ladies are appalled by what they read, they can close the book at the bottom of page one; if they read further, they will learn what is in the world and in its people, and no parents who have been discerning with their children need fear the outcome. Nor can they hold it back, for life is a series of little battles and minor issues, and the burden of choice is on us all, every day, young and old. Our daughters must live in the world and decide what sort of women they are to be, and we should be willing to prefer their deliberate and informed choice of decency rather than an innocence that continues to spring from ignorance. If that choice be made in the open sunlight, it is more apt than when made in shadow to fall on the side of honorable behavior.

I predict that, if special pressures against books and their expanding position in our cultural life are increased, we shall go through a very uncomfortable period of group tensions. In the long run, in a free country, the censor cannot win. Those who attempt to play the role of censor will reap the whirlwind of public reaction. The good people of our country will never, in my opinion, forfeit a fundamental liberty in order to correct a temporary condition.

A DISTRIBUTOR'S WARNING [10]

Unfortunately, so much controversy has raged about the pocket-sized novels, the comic books, and magazines of this suggestive and undesirable type that it is hard to separate the facts from the feelings that now are so inflamed. The attacks that have been made upon newsdealers and distributors have aroused the deepest anxieties of parents and civic leaders.

The critics spend their time and energy in pointing out the horrible examples. They do not reassure the parents and the community by admitting that not all books and magazines are bad, or by pointing out that it is the exceptional, and not the average child or adolescent who, for whatever cause, lapses into delinquency. . . .

It is true, Dr. [Mandel] Sherman [University of Chicago psychologist] points out, that a child may ascribe his behavior to a comic book or magazine that he has read or to a movie that he has seen, but such explanations cannot be considered scientific evidence of causation.

The causes of juvenile delinquency and crime are far more complex. They are deeply rooted in unhappy home life, in poverty-ridden slums, in the lack of sufficient playgrounds and in other failures of our society to meet the basic needs of our children and our young people.

Thus our consciences may rest easy on that score. As distributors of pocket-sized novels, comic books and magazines, we are not contributing to juvenile delinquency and crime. This does not solve our problem, however, for it arises not because of what

[10] From "This Literature We Distribute," address by Samuel Black, vice president, to the Atlantic Coast Independent Distributors Association annual convention, Hollywood Beach, Florida, April 25, 1952. In Report of the House of Representatives Select Committee on Current Pornographic Materials. 82d Congress, 2d session. Superintendent of Documents, Washington 25, D.C. 1952. p 131-4. Reprinted by permission.

we do, but because of what people think. And make no mistake about it.

If the publishers and distributors of newsstand literature do not do something about this problem themselves, the state, under public pressure, will adopt a solution that could lead to the ruination of all of us. . . .

Frankly, there is no real justification or excuse for much of the material we are distributing. It is imperative that we free ourselves, without delay, from the constant fear that haunts us every time we put out a pocket-size book which causes one to wonder what manner of diseased mind can contrive such tripe; with covers that continually are becoming more and more revealing, and in many instances have little or no relation to, or bearing upon, the subject matter. . . .

Instead of a limited distribution, these books are displayed not only in the eighteen hundred book stores of the country but in over ninety thousand retail neighborhood and drug stores, and probably starts off with a print schedule of three hundred thousand as against twenty thousand total for the original edition.

There has been a change in the reading and buying habits of the nation, and the reprint publishers must be made to realize their obligation to this vast public. The youth of the country must be respected, not corrupted, as is the case with much of the material now spewing from the presses—and I say "spewing" without any reservation.

I have quoted action being taken by the Federal Government. State governments are also active, and the city fathers are breathing hot air down our necks. What must happen before the publishers wake up to the fact they are killing everything that is good in the publishing business? And what are we going to do if this tremendous business is not to be driven from pillar to post and then destroyed—destroyed by the greed of some publishers for a fast dollar? . . .

After devoting much thought and reflection to this whole problem of the literature we distribute, I have come to some conclusions. . . . It seems to me that this is the sort of problem with which we distributors, if we attempt to meet it as individuals, are helpless to cope. On the other hand, I see no reason why we could not make a real and substantial contribution to its solution if we handle it through our association. . . .

One of the results of this convention, I believe, should be the establishment of a committee charged with the task of working out a definite plan and program with the publishers for remedying a condition of which none of us is proud.

The details of such a program should be worked out by this committee on the basis of suggestions from us, the members of this association, and those publishers who are concerned with the welfare of the industry rather than for selfish interests. . . .

One of our members offered this thought: American reading habits have changed, for Americans are now reading hundreds of millions of pocket-sized books and even more billions of magazines. This is a public trust and responsibility of which we must be fully cognizant—one we must never forget. Reading is now enjoyed by the entire nation, and not by just a privileged few. Who has made this possible? Many people, not the least however, being the independent distributor wholesaler, for it is through us that the great volume of reading matter, most of it good and wholesome and informative, is widely and efficiently distributed.

This represents an accomplishment on the part of our business as a whole that the public is not completely aware of; otherwise it would not forget it so quickly when a storm breaks over one of the objectionable minority. Nevertheless, the evil, no matter how small, is very serious and must be dealt with. It is incumbent upon us to take the kind of action necessary to combat it—immediately; even here—today.

APPEAL TO BOOKSELLERS [11]

Our fiction today shows what we have been through: our novels reflect the suffering of the depression; they show the neu-

[11] From "The American Public Trusts the Bookseller," address by Edward A. Weeks, editor, *Atlantic Monthly*, before American Booksellers Association convention, Chicago, May 25, 1953. *Publishers' Weekly*. 163:2384-6. June 6, 1953. Reprinted by permission.

rotic tendencies traced by Freud; they show the brutality of concentration camps and the violence of two world wars. These are the facts of the life we have survived and we cannot conceal them from our children. But we can ask that our publishers raise their sights and respect our standards instead of pandering to the pulp market. We can show our disgust with the bosomy, blowsy novel whose heroine—to judge from the jacket—is always undressing or being undressed.

We can ask that the paper-backed reprints do not change the titles to make books seem more lurid than they are: to change a book originally entitled *The Nutmeg Tree* to *Julia Misbehaves,* or another called originally *American Earth* to *A Swell Looking Girl* is silly; it is lurid and it invites reprisals. This is a prime example of editorial misreading of the public.

I travel this country thirty thousand miles a year and since 1947 I have noticed a rising tide of vigilance: Americans are more vigilant about national defense, more vigilant about our resources, our loyalty and our community life. Ideas and morals are both under scrutiny. There is evidence of this vigilance in the openly circulated blacklists.

In this wave of vigilance there are zealots who would have the Federal Government or the church act as censor. But there is no sanity in that notion; the very idea is repugnant to our American heritage. You can see what a "czar" does to books and freedom of speech in Moscow, Spain and Argentina.

No, our best hope is in plain speaking and in voluntary action. You booksellers must speak out in defense of worthy books and return lurid books to the publisher. The public has always trusted you and if you are forthright it will continue to. You know your natural allies: the publishers, librarians, Parent-Teacher associations, League of Women Voters, American Association of University Women, above all, the law courts. The law is really our last big resort in this fight. I am very proud of Judge Goldman of New Jersey who ruled that it was against the Constitution to set up a local censor [Bantam Books case against Matthew F. Melco, former prosecuting attorney of Middlesex County, *Publishers' Weekly,* April 11]. If you are subject to pressure groups or bigots, you can arouse the conscientious spirit in your community. In this crisis we need to have better books, less trash, and more trust in the taste of American readers. To the zealots who would stiffen the laws I give Thomas Jefferson's great truth: "Our liberty depends on the freedom of the press and that cannot be limited without being lost."

HOW POLICE CENSORS WORK [12]

Inspector Case: A literary censor was established in the Detroit Police Department in 1937. This group was absorbed by the detective bureau in 1941, and in 1948 a separate group was created to handle the problem.

Mr. Burton [H. Ralph Burton, committee counsel]: What was it that precipitated the creation of a special bureau to handle these matters?

Mr. Case: Well, in the beginning we had these stands which were completely saturated with questionable materials, sexed-up covers and so on, and the great number of complaints we had received necessitated the organization of such a specific bureau. . . .

Mr. Burton: What was the final result of this comic-book situation; were the distributors or the dealers prosecuted?

Mr. Case: . . . Let me explain it this way: We have about three hundred—at that time we had pretty close to 380 titles of comic books being distributed in the metropolitan area. . . . I think it will run pretty close to 2.25 million comic books that were being distributed. . . . Of course we had many specific cases where they displayed or portrayed crimes and the criminal, glorified crime, bloodshed, lust and especially tortures of various types.

We had the parents and various groups come to us with complaints, and it was necessary that we screen these 380 titles, with the ultimate result that we had about eighty of those that we submitted to the Wayne County prosecuting attorney's office. . . .

12 From testimony by Inspector Herbert W. Case, Detroit Police License and Censor Bureau, December 2, 1952. In Report of the House of Representatives Select Committee on Current Pornographic Materials. 82d Congress, 2d session. Superintendent of Documents. Washington 25, D.C. 1952. p50-63.

I think there were forty-eight that were judged definitely by the prosecuting attorney to be a violation of our state statute.

We then informed the distributor . . . who in turn notified the publisher, that they were in violation of our state statute, that they would have to be withheld from circulation, or they could be defended in court. . . . The result was that they were withheld.

Mr. Burton: . . . What were the long-range effects that resulted from this situation?

Mr Case: . . . Some of the publishers sent in advance copies to us. . . . They did make a lot of deletions; they cleaned up a lot of them to the point where the complaints did drop down. . . .

Mr. Burton: Is it not true, Inspector, that if you pursued the other method it would be a much longer effort on your part, because each book would have to be considered, would it not?

Mr. Case: Oh, yes; by all means.

Mr. Burton: By the courts?

Mr. Case: That is correct.

Mr. Burton: Why do you feel these publications that you have been discussing, such as the pocket-size books and the comics, present such a problem?

Mr. Case: Well, we have two or three specific reasons for that. First of all, it is a low price. A few years back you had your average hard-cover book which sold at anywhere from two dollars on up, and then after it had its run more or less they brought it out into cheaper editions in the chain organizations, but they were quite careful, to a certain extent they were, as to what they distributed.

Now, it is out in the twenty-five-cent book. It is placed out, easily obtainable by the youth and, as I have often said, we in the municipality feel that the law and the statutes and everything are intended to protect the adolescent, the weak and susceptible. That is primarily our objective on it, and to strike at the source of supply, so when these low prices make it available, it is circulated in what we call unlimited distribution. It is in the confectionery stores across from the schools, across from the playgrounds, the drug stores, and in Detroit we did have 2,500 retail outlets. . . .

Mr. Burton: And that occurs throughout the United States?

Mr Case: That occurs; yes, sir. We feel that is definitely in every city and hamlet in the country. . . .

Mr. Burton: Do you have any suggestions as to what might be done in order to correct the problem of obscene material? . . .

Mr. Case: The publishers themselves have got to get together and, as I said, they are going to have to bring into the fold the unscrupulous few who you definitely know are a menace to the entire country. . . .

It appears to me personally that they have reached a crossroads, it seems as the movie industry did years ago. They got together when they were faced with this; they got their heads together, and probably the movie industry today is the most highly policed industry in the world. . . . I think the publishers can go a long way, if they want to.

Mr. Burton: Do you feel that the Detroit system for dealing with questionable magazines and pocket-size books could be utilized in other communities?

Mr. Case: There is no question about it. . . . But there are a lot of police departments in the smaller communities that do not have the manpower. . . . We are only too glad to cooperate. . . .

Mr. Burton: Inspector, in your many years of police experience, have you observed any correlation between pornographic material and criminology?

Mr. Case: Well, yes. I have very conscientiously watched this. I have yet to see a sex murder case in the history of the Detroit Police Department but what I can show you obscene literature, either of the commercial type or of his own creation.

THE ISSUE IN YOUNGSTOWN [13]

Early this year Edward S. Allen, the Police Chief of Youngstown, Ohio, started a campaign against the sale of obscene and indecent literature. As part of the campaign he prepared a list of 108 paper-bound books and 33 magazines. The list was sent to

[13] From "Due Process," editorial. *Commonweal.* 58:505. August 28, 1953. Reprinted by permission.

Bernard Bloch, local distributor of the books, requesting that he remove them from all newsstands. Failure to comply with this request, Allen said, would result in arrest and prosecution of the distributor or any dealers who "display or sell their periodicals." Among the books listed were three novels by James T. Farrell and two by Alberto Moravia. They and the others were removed.

The New American Library, publisher of eleven of the books in question, then brought suit against Chief Allen and the City of Youngstown. The plaintiff alleged that the ordinance under which the books had been banned was unconstitutional, and that in banning them the chief of police had transcended his powers.

In August a Federal court reached a decision in the case. In it Judge McNamee upheld the constitutionality of Youngstown's anti-obscenity ordinance but declared that in acting as a self-appointed censor the police chief had indeed transcended his power. Enforcement of such an ordinance, the judge said, must follow due process.

In a case such as this due process was flagrantly violated.

Not only did the defendant exceed his lawful powers in suppressing the publications, [Judge McNamee declared], but the methods be employed in censoring the books were arbitrary and unreasonable. This is not to impugn the defendant's sincerity of purpose or his praiseworthy ambition to suppress lewd and indecent literature. But a chief of police, like all other public officials, must act within the scope of his express and implied powers under the law.

Arbitrary power inspired by good motives, no less than that motivated by evil intent, is an attack upon the supremacy of the law. It is of the utmost importance to prevent the distribution of all forms of indecent and lewd literature with its demoralizing effects upon the young. It is vital in the interest of public morality that the laws against obscenity be vigorously enforced. But if a free society is to endure, its primary obligation is to protect its government of laws against all intrusions of arbitrary power.

These words deserve wide quotation. They are a concise statement of the real point at issue in numerous cases of this kind. The right of a community to protect itself by law against the distribution of obscenity should be obvious. It should be equally obvious that the question of whether or not a particular book is, indeed, obscene must be decided in court after the testimony of competent witnesses has been heard.

The question of what books should be banned cannot be left to the determination of police officials or private groups, no matter how laudable their intentions may be. That way lies chaos and the death of freedom. Judge McNamee's decision set right an intolerable local situation, but it could serve as a model for other American cities faced with a similar problem.

THE THREAT OF VIGILANTES [14]

Extralegal attacks on sellers of "objectionable" literature seem to be spreading. One of the centers of these attacks is in Minneapolis, where this form of cultural Ku Kluxism has encountered formidable opposition, including that of the Minneapolis *Star*, one of the nation's best newspapers. The method is evidently intended to accomplish by threats what cannot be done by law. It operates as follows:

Drugstores and newsstands receive letters from a self-constituted "citizens' committee" calling for removal of "all objectionable literature" and threatening police action against those who do not cooperate. Then clergymen also receive from this committee letters asking their support of the prospective drive. The letter to the vendors quotes the city ordinance concerning obscene printed matter and says a committee will call with a list of the material which must be banned.

The *Star* reports that a buyer for a chain of Minnesota drugstores got a list of "objectionable" books from the chairman of the citizens' committee. The list was entitled, "Publications which do not conform to the code of the National Organization for Decent Literature," a Roman Catholic organization which is the counterpart in this field of the Legion of Decency in movie censorship.

Authors of banned books include Nobel Prize winner William Faulkner, James T. Farrell, Somerset Maugham, Lillian

[14] From "Vigilante Censorship Is Spreading," editorial. *Chairman Century.* 70:404. April 8, 1953. Reprinted by permission.

Smith and Richard Wright. The contents of these books do not come under the intent of the laws against obscenity as they are usually interpreted. But the threat of police action almost always frightens the vendor into withdrawing these books from circulation. Such persons almost always refuse to stand on their rights and test the issue in court.

So self-appointed vigilantes actually come into power over the reading habits of the community, and rule by a terroristic censorship that operates outside the law. It may be assumed that some of the books to which these cultural storm troopers object are morally corrupt, but the harm they could do if permitted to circulate freely is not one tenth as great as that wrought by the blight which is spread over American democracy by these methods of intimidation.

POLITICAL CENSORSHIP

EDITOR'S INTRODUCTION

"No arguments, we may suppose, can now be needed against permitting a legislature or an executive, not identified in interest with the people, to prescribe opinions to them, and determine what doctrines or what arguments they shall be allowed to hear." So John Stuart Mill observed in the chapter of his essay *On Liberty,* quoted earlier in this volume.

Mill could not have forseen the "cold war" of the current generation. He could not, apparently, conceive of an era in which the question of subversive influences would pervade every phase of a nation's life. Irene Corbally Kuhn's crusade against "books that sell communism," which opens this section, raised this question in the realm of books. In the following selection a former Communist challenges the assumption that Communists and fellow-travelers dominated the book world in the so-called "Red Decade"—the 1930's.

The initiator of "book-labeling" in San Antonio, Texas, explains the aims and methods of that campaign, inspired by a fifteen-year-old military school cadet whose suggestion was incorporated in a bill introduced in the Texas Legislature. A free-lance writer tells how a group of San Antonio citizens mobilized to resist the "labelers."

President Eisenhower's "Don't-join-the-book-burners" speech sounds a keynote of warning against those who would impose on schools and libraries their own criteria of "safe" reading. Finally, an author and teacher replies to a school board that banned his books because it did not approve his political associations.

BOOK REVIEWERS AND COMMUNISM [1]

At its highest point, about 1938, the Comintern (it's now the Cominform), as the international Communist organization was

[1] From "Why You Buy Books That Sell Communism," by Irene Corbally Kuhn, contributing editor, *American Mercury. American Legion Magazine.* 50:18+. January 1951. Reprinted by permission.

known, had mobilized the deliberately conscious or the starry-eyed innocent collaboration of thousands of influential American educators, New Deal officials, social workers, Social Registerites, novelists, script writers, directors, publishers, editors and the literati generally. Each phase of American life and activity could be explored almost endlessly for proof of the success of this sinister foreign propaganda that has but one aim: the destruction of free, capitalist society and the conversion of thinking, independent men and women into plodding mindless slaves.

It is with but one phase of this intellectual cuckoldry of the Kremlin that we can deal in this article—the penetration of the book-publishing field and its essential attribute, literary reviewing and criticism. . . .

The importance of the reviewer . . . is evident, since the only news the public gets of a book is through the reviews, and paid advertising; and paid advertising, more often than not, depends on the amount, kind and quality of the reviews. If the reviews are poor, the publisher won't put money into paid advertising. He can't afford to. He can afford it less if the book gets no reviews, which often happens. Depending also on the reviews is the extent of the sales effort expended on the book. Before the reviewer has given his verdict, the bookseller has had information about the book only from the publisher's representative, the naturally prejudiced salesman, and a few other trade sources. No bookseller, not even the most industrious and conscientious ones, can read all the eight thousand to ten thousand new books that come out every year. He has to depend on reviewers' estimates of books more than on his own judgment and experience. . . .

The Communists were the first to see this, naturally, so it was imperative that if they were to control or dominate this important field of communications, they spot their agents or sympathizers among the reviewers. Thorough strategists that they are, they don't rely on partial or even complete coverage of a single arm; they make use of the whole body of publishing.

In addition to spotting their agents or sympathizers among the reviewers, they actually get active party members or cooperative fellow-travelers into publishing houses as editors or editorial assistants; they put their people into retail book outlets, in department stores and bookshops.

And they have set up and control book selling clubs, related trade unions, etc. And, of course, the party has plenty of members always ready to follow the line in fiction or nonfiction work; to logroll for the other faithful, and to be hatchet men against anti-Communist writers.

Thus organized, they are able to work a parallel course of intensive propaganda for their aims and sabotage of everyone and everything opposed to those aims.

Whenever a book comes along that is potentially damaging to the Communist effort, the entire strength of their forces is marshaled against it. They go beyond just book reviews; they bear down on the faithful and the naïve in all other specialized types of writing; syndicated columns, editorials, etc., for it is through this group that public opinion is formed, convictions cemented, prejudices solidified and hatreds whipped up.

Just this past summer, the syndicated columnist, Bob Considine, one of the country's best and most prolific writers, and a fearless one who calls the shots as he sees them, spoke about this field of specialized writing, which is his own, on a national radio network. . . :

> If there is any apparent anti-religious feeling among these specialists in journalism, it will be found chiefly among the book reviews of certain leading New York newspapers and literary publications.
>
> Here a rather shocking situation prevails. If you write a book which steps on the toes of our home-grown left-wingers, bamboozled liberals or outright Communists, or their idols abroad, you can almost count on receiving a number of sour reviews—where the reviews hurt most.

Sometimes the attack centers on the author, regardless of the book. John T. Flynn is one such victim, and the violence of the attack on him was all the greater because experience had shown that Mr. Flynn, with a long-established reputation as a writer, editor, critic and fighter for principle, didn't scare easily and never quit. When he wrote *The Roosevelt Myth* [1948], he submitted the manuscript to several publishers and discussed it with still others. This was the first time in his more than forty years' experience as a well-known writer-editor that he had had to "peddle" a book manuscript. . . .

Mr. Flynn found a courageous publisher in young Devin Garrity, head of the firm of Devin-Adair. . . .

Mr. Flynn's [next] book, *The Road Ahead* [1949] by all the criteria applied to books, should have had the widest attention from reviewers, especially in the nationally circulated Sunday book review supplements.

At this point Mr. Devin Garrity reports:

> We published the book and waited for the reviews, especially the Sunday New York *Herald Tribune*. After two months, when it seemed fairly certain there would be no review, I instituted some inquiries and learned that the review copy [of the book] had been received and was on file, but that it had been marked for the silent treatment. No review was scheduled for it.
>
> We then bought advertising space in the *Herald Tribune's* Sunday book section and ran the excellent and fair review of Mr. Flynn's book which had been written by John Chamberlain and published in *Human Events*, a small Washington, D.C., publication. . . .
>
> The *Herald Tribune* then changed its position, probably as a result of the ad, because in three weeks . . . a review did appear—a smear job to counteract the effect of the favorable Chamberlain review we had bought the space to run.

For a perfect example of the all-out, four-alarm attack on an anti-Communist book by another well-known anti-Communist author, W. L. White's *Report on the Russians* is probably the classic example. . . .

The White book, recounting his trip through Russia [with Eric Johnston], was published by Harcourt, Brace [in 1945], after condensation in the *Reader's Digest*. . . . Where the publishers had confidently expected, and with good reason, that it would sell 120,000 copies, the total was some 40,000 less. . . .

The book was so abused and the Stalinist operation against it so comprehensive that reviewers for libraries and church organizations were suggesting, "Don't read this; it's a prejudiced book." . . .

One of the hatchet men on Mr. White's book was Edgar Snow, long-time writer-editor for the *Saturday Evening Post*, and a signer of the petition condemning Mr. White's book. Mr. Snow has long been on good terms with the left. . . . The *Saturday Review of Literature* chose Mr. Snow to do the job on George Creel's . . . book, *Russia's Race for Asia* [1949], and Snow produced a highly unfair review. . . .

Mr. Creel had another sample of this when the New York *Times* turned his *Russia's Race for Asia* over for review to Professor Nathaniel Peffer of Columbia University, a frequent contributor to the *Times* Sunday Magazine Section and its Sunday Book Section. Professor Peffer has been an unremitting foe of Nationalist China and Chiang Kai-shek in virtually everything he has written since the Japanese surrender. . . .

The American people had no real knowledge of China. The leftists filled the vacuum with their own books, reviewed favorably by each other. . . .

Guenther Stein . . . in 1945 brought out *The Challenge of Red China*. This book was reviewed in the New York *Times* by the aforesaid Nathaniel Peffer. . . .

John K. Fairbank, Harvard professor . . . in 1948 wrote a book titled *The United States and China*, published by the Harvard University Press. . . .

On the jacket of Professor Fairbank's tome was Theodore H. White's assertion that this was "the best one-volume job on China I've ever read." Mr. White, formerly *Time-Life* correspondent, was only thirty-two years of age at the time, with nine years' residence in war-time Chungking and no time at all in China when it wasn't at war. With Annalee Jacoby . . . he wrote *Thunder out of China* [1946], . . . [an] all-out attack on Chiang Kai-shek and the Nationalist Government. . . .

Professor Fairbank's book was praised equally highly by the late Richard Lauterbach with a really fulsome statement, and by Owen Lattimore, with more brevity but with the same enthusiasm.

Now for Fairbank the reviewer, as we logroll along.

He was given three books on China to review for the Sunday Book Section of the New York *Times*. He returned the

White-Jacoby compliment when he reviewed their book, *Thunder out of China.* . . .

On February 9, 1947, Mr. Fairbank reviewed two other books for the *Times, China's Destiny,* by Chiang Kai-shek, an edition authorized by the author; and an edited, unauthorized edition of the same book prepared by Philip Jaffe. Fairbank reviewed these together and managed to say nothing about Jaffe's known bias for the pro-Communist cause in China, nor of his involvement in the *Amerasia* case in which Jaffe was fined for participation in the theft of secret documents from the State Department. . . .

For more logjamming, Mrs. Jacoby appeared in the New York *Times* Sunday Book Section on December 19, 1946, as the reviewer of *My Twenty-Five Years in China,* by John B. Powell, an American of unquestioned integrity who lost both his feet in a Japanese prison. . . . Mrs. Jacoby berates the author as a "reactionary" and insists that peace in China's Civil War depends on "progress in negotiations between the Kuomintang and the Communists." . . .

When another non-Communist book, this time on Japan, *Japan and the Son of Heaven,* by Willard De Mille Price, was reviewed in the *Times* of October 14, 1945, the reviewer was none other than Owen Lattimore, who criticized the book unfavorably.

When Lattimore's own book, *Solution in Asia,* was reviewed in the February 25, 1945, issue, Edgar Snow was given the task. . . .

Two weeks later in the issue of March 11, 1945, the *Times* again lent the book review columns to that annoyingly persistent combination: a pro-Commie book on China, reviewed, of course, by Edgar Snow. This time more than a full page was devoted to Harrison Forman's book, *Report from Red China.* . . . Harrison Forman, the author of this book, is an explorer, lecturer and newsreel man who had made films of the Chinese Communists. . . .

The fact that the New York *Times* book reviewing activities have been specifically examined at some length in this article should not be construed as an indictment of that paper alone. The New York *Herald Tribune* in both its daily section and its Sunday supplement . . . presents abundant evidence of favoritism of the left. . . .

Lewis Gannett, the book review editor and literary critic of the *Herald Tribune* is himself an excellent writer, an experienced reviewer who is also an influential voice in the expression of *Herald Tribune* policy and a protagonist of many causes. . . .

Mr. Gannett has never reviewed *Seeds of Treason*, the Victor Lasky-Ralph de Toledano book on the trials of Alger Hiss, although its value and importance and distinct literary merit and interest are unquestioned and its pre-publication publicity was extraordinary. The book has been on the best-seller lists despite this and other attempts to keep it out of the public eye.

On the other hand, *Ordeal by Slander*, by Owen Lattimore, a "quickie" done by the man Senator Joe McCarthy accuses of being the chief architect of our disastrous Far Eastern policy, got extra-special treatment from both the *Herald Tribune* and New York *Times*.

The two papers published on two successive days, Sunday, July 30 and Monday, July 31, a big blast of favorable publicity vindicating Mr. Lattimore and damning Joe McCarthy. This was not done in the news columns; the book columns obliged. Both gave *Ordeal by Slander* all of page one of their Sunday book review sections, plus a breakover; and each followed this with a lavish plug for the defense with another burst of cheering next morning in the daily review columns.

The *Herald Tribune* Sunday review was done by John K. Fairbank. . . . His choice to review *Ordeal by Slander* is particularly brazen because on page 203 of the book Lattimore related how Fairbank aided him in advance of his appearance before the Congressional Committee [on un-American Activities]. "John Fairbank of Harvard sent out telegrams to a long list of Far Eastern experts all over the country, suggesting that they write Senator Tydings, the chairman of the committee," protesting, naturally.

DID REDS DOMINATE THE BOOK BUSINESS? [2]

As a Communist in the thirties, I felt, and rejoiced to feel, that I belonged to a movement that was growing in power. Thanks to the Depression, the party had greatly increased its membership and, even more greatly, its influence, and its influence continued to grow during the entire period, 1935-1939, in which I was a member. Yet as a writer, a publisher's adviser, and a teacher, I was never conscious of the kind of power in the intellectual world that John Chamberlain [former editor of the *Freeman*] attributes to the Communists. Far from capturing "the word capital of the United States," we won only small and precarious victories.

Let me tell of what I know, beginning with the publishing business. I suppose that in the thirties almost every publishing house in the country had at least one Communist or Communist sympathizer on its staff. In many instances the political views of these men and women were known to their colleagues and superiors; in others they were suspected; in others they were more or less successfully kept secret.

It is also true that many books sympathetic to communism were published in these years, and frequently, I am sure, it was a Communist editor who brought in a Communist book. It is fatuous, however, to conclude that these books were always, or even as a general rule, "put over" by these editors. What some people are able to forget is that there was a market for left-wing books in the thirties. One need not postulate a Communist conspiracy, for example, to explain why Covici Friede published John Strachey's *The Coming Struggle for Power*; in the atmosphere of 1933 the book was bound to be popular. The firm of John Day, cooperating with the *New Masses* in offering a prize for the best proletarian novel, was a victim not of a conspiracy but of an illusion that proletarian novels would sell. When Harper and Brothers published the early books of Richard Wright, when Harcourt, Brace published Ella Winter's *Red*

² From "How Red Was the Red Decade?" by Granville Hicks, former Communist, writer on American social and intellectual history. *Harper's Magazine.* 207:53-61. July 1953. Reprinted by permission.

Virtue, when Doubleday, Doran published *Red Medicine* by Sir Arthur Newsholme and John A. Kingsbury, when Random House published Angelo Herndon's *Let Me Live,* when Knopf published Agnes Smedley's books on China, these eminent firms were simply behaving like publishers.

The Macmillan Company published my book, *The Great Tradition,* in 1933, with full awareness that it purported to be a Marxist study of American literature. In 1935 they not only brought out a revised edition that was even more explicitly Communist but brought it out in cooperation with International Publishers, the official Communist publishing house. In 1936 Macmillan published my *John Reed,* a biography of a Communist by a Communist, and were happy to have it selected by the Book Union, a book club whose Communist leanings were obvious to everyone. And during all this time the president of the company was an outspoken conservative, and none of the editors, so far as I ever discovered, was a Communist or a Communist sympathizer.

I know something about the situation at Macmillan in the thirties, for I was one of the firm's literary advisers. Naturally my judgments were influenced by the fact that I was a Communist, and this was taken for granted by the editors. It was so definitely taken for granted that I couldn't have put anything over. I recommended a certain number of books that were sympathetic to communism, but I recommended them for what they were and on the grounds that they would sell. I also recommended, on the same grounds, some anti-Communist books, including Arthur Koestler's first novel, *The Gladiators.* On the other hand, the company published at least one Communist book—Henri Barbusse's *Stalin*—that I never saw until it was in print.

The policy that I followed in my work for Macmillan was, I like to think, a matter of integrity, but it was also plain common sense. After all, an editor or adviser who recommends a series of unsuccessful books, whether out of bias or out of bad judgment, doesn't last long. For that reason, Communists in other publishing firms were obliged to adhere generally to the same policy, whether they liked it or not. "Infiltrees," as John

Chamberlain calls them, were probably responsible for some of the pro-Communist books published in the thirties, but they accomplished less than he thinks—and less, I am sure, than they thought at the time.

As people forgot then and forget now, it is one thing to get a book published and another to get it read, as the fantastic story of Modern Age Books shows. This firm, which was founded to publish both reprints and original books in paper-bound editions, was financed by Richard S. Childs, who, to the best of my belief, was not a party member but was scarcely a militant anti-Communist. Its pioneering experiment in publishing paper-bound books, an enterprise that became so spectacularly successful in other hands, proved a failure, partly because there wasn't sufficient study and preparation but also because the Communists took the firm over.

Modern Age did a lot for the Communists. Heaven knows how many it employed in one capacity or another, and some substantial advances fell into Communist hands. Moreover, many party-line books were published. Some of these, including my own *I Like America*, did fairly well, but the majority were flops. Even when the party pushed them for all it was worth, they would not move. Childs poured in money, but the firm tottered and fell, and a lot of loyal Communists went looking for jobs. . . .

If there were such a house in existence today, I would denounce it as promptly and as heartily as I would have denounced a Fascist concern in 1939—or would denounce one today. Yet it would be easy to exaggerate the evil that Modern Age was able to accomplish. If some of its books may have had a wide influence, most of them, I believe, were bought almost exclusively by people who were already convinced Communists. And the company was ruined, in no great length of time, by its Communist activities.

In *The Red Decade* [1941] Eugene Lyons has a chapter called "Intellectual Red Terror," in which he argues that pressure was used to prevent the publication of anti-Communist books and that such books, if they appeared, were attacked and vilified. I know of only one attempt to suppress a book, and Mr. Lyons mentions only one, and they happen to be the same: a concerted effort, in which I refused to take part, was made to try to persuade Viking Press not to publish Benjamin Stolberg's *Story of the C.I.O.* [1938]. It failed. Perhaps there were other attempts that succeeded, but the fact remains that many anti-Communist books were published in the thirties, none more successfully than Mr. Lyons' *Assignment in Utopia* [1939]. All the writers he mentions as victims of the intellectual red terror— John Dewey, Max Eastman, Ben Stolberg, James Farrell, John Dos Passos, William Henry Chamberlain, etc.—found publishers in the thirties. Nor was Lyons the only writer who was able to express his disillusionment with the Soviet Union; he himself speaks of Andrew Smith, Fred Beal, Jan Valtin, Freda Utley, and the Tchernavins.

Of course these books were attacked in the Communist press, in language as virulent as that employed by Mr. Lyons. And in the heyday of the Popular Front there were, as he says, strategically placed reviewers who, if not Communists, tended to reflect the Communist line. But it was not my impression then, and it is not my impression now, that the Communists had things their own way. I wrote an article for the *New Masses* of October 2, 1934, in which I argued, with considerable evidence, that the New York *Times Book Review* assigned almost all books on Russia to anti-Communists, usually Russian enemies of the Soviet regime. I further pointed out that the editor and several of the principal reviewers consistently went out of their way to sneer at and belittle American writers known to be sympathetic to communism. Mr. Lyons can call my article part of the "intellectual red terror" if he wants to, but no one will deny that the *Times* had more influence in the world of books than the *New Masses*.

Some time later (December 7, 1937) I wrote an article on the book reviews in the *Nation*. . . . Pro-Communist books, I pointed out, were given to such reviewers as Abram Harris, Edmund Wilson, Ben Stolberg, Louis Hacker, Sterling Spero, Susanne LaFollette, Anita Brenner, James Rorty, Philip Rahv,

Sidney Hook, and James Burnham, all of whom could be counted on not to like them. The *Nation's* book review section was an organ for those anti-Communists who, according to Mr. Lyons, had such a bad time.

We felt—make no mistake about it—that we were the victims, that we were the ones who were being persecuted. The big magazines, those that paid good money, were notoriously hostile not only to communism and the Soviet Union but virtually to all the ideas advocated by the Popular Front. An individual writer for one of these magazines might be a Communist sympathizer, but he was both smart and lucky if he got away with any propaganda. Kyle Crichton, for instance, a staff writer for *Collier's*, saved his radical ideas for the articles he wrote for the *New Masses* under the name of Robert Forsythe; he did not try to put them over in *Collier's*. . . .

Many Communist teachers, I am sure, went just as far as they could in presenting the Communist view of their subjects, but few of them were so situated that they could go very far. How much influence they had on their students is anybody's guess, except that it was much less than is supposed. . . . There were many students in the thirties who joined the Young Communist League or belonged to one or another of the party fronts. Some of them, I am sure, were influenced by Communist teachers, but for the most part they were responding to the same influences as the teachers were. Communism was in the air, and a certain number of people were bound to catch it. . . .

Disillusionment is a phenomenon that has not been sufficiently examined. As I have pointed out, most of the men who are responsible for the myth of the Red Decade—and most of the highly articulate anti-Communists in general—were themselves, for at least brief periods, under Communist influence. They recovered, and so did a larger proportion of their associates than they are willing to admit.

The fact that so many intellectuals have been disillusioned suggests that a lot of them were not very good Communists to begin with. The public has been educated by extracts from the writings of Lenin and Stalin to an understanding of what membership in the Communist party is supposed to mean, and the autobiographies of such persons as Whittaker Chambers and Elizabeth Bentley, who tried hard to be good Communists, have helped to create a picture of the perfectly disciplined party member, ready to obey without hesitation any command his superiors may give him. That is unquestionably the party ideal, but it is an ideal to which many Communists do not measure up, and in the later thirties, when it was seeking a respectable façade, the party did not even attempt to impose this ideal upon the intellectuals. Therefore, even if it can be shown that there were so many party members at such and such a time in such and such an institution, it does not follow that there were that many docile agents of the Soviet Union. Some of these people, if the party had tried to use them as agents, would have quit on the spot, and the party knew it.

To say all this is not to extenuate the mistakes made by the intellectuals, myself included, who swallowed communism. I am saying that we were suckers, and to a great extent we were, but it is no defense whatever for an intellectual to say that he was duped, since that is what, as an intellectual, he should never allow to happen to him. We were taken in by ideas we should have seen through and people we should have suspected. And, being writers and publicists, we proceeded to take in other people, which is why the party was willing to bother with us in the first place. There is no telling how much damage I may have done, and though I have tried hard in the past fourteen years to undo it, I am by no means sure that I have succeeded.

Nor am I suggesting that communism should be taken lightly today. Communism has never been so thoroughly discredited in the United States as it is right now, and if we could think purely in national terms, it would be nothing to worry about, but we have to think in terms of the the world situation, and Communists as actual or potential agents of a hostile power are a danger not to be scoffed at. We must constantly be on the alert to meet their propaganda, and, as a nation, we must be able to combat their espionage and sabotage. If the danger is sometimes exaggerated, it is nevertheless a danger.

All I am trying to do is to destroy a myth. In his contribution to *Socialism and American Life*, one of the most careful students of the subject, Daniel Bell, writes: "Although communism never won a mass following in the United States, it did have a disproportionate influence in the cultural field. At one time, from 1936 to 1939, through the fellow-travelers in the publishing houses, radio, Hollywood, the magazines, and other mass media, it exercised influence on public opinion far beyond the mere number of party members." That, I think, is absolutely true, but although the influence of the party undoubtedly was disproportionate to its membership, it was not unlimited. The notion that communism dominated American culture in the thirties is false.

The notion has to be corrected, not only to keep the record straight but also to counteract the damage the myth of the Red Decade is doing to our national morale. Every time somebody says, "Boy, the Reds nearly got us in the thirties," his listeners shiver, thinking, "It might happen again." The significant, the hopeful point, as Frederick Lewis Allen suggests in *The Big Change*, is that it never did happen. Even in the early thirties, when millions of people were hungry and desperate, the Communists barely polled a hundred thousand votes. Even in the later thirties, when the Popular Front had captured the allegiance of many intellectuals, they made little impression on the solid anti-communism of the great majority of the American people. Even when it tried to disguise itself as twentieth-century Americanism, communism could not count more than a few hundred thousand sympathizers. A hundred thousand disciplined Communists might be something to think twice about, but most sympathizers were as far from the Leninist ideal as most church-goers are from the Christian ideal, and they soon found plenty of reason for backsliding.

That communism should seem thoroughly evil to most Americans today is natural enough. What is encouraging is that it seemed highly unattractive to all but a handful fifteen and twenty years ago, when our system appeared to be on the skids and when much less was known than is known now about Communist tyranny and aggression. Fifteen years ago I would have asserted that the American attitude towards communism was a result of misinformation and prejudice, and certainly it wasn't a purely rational thing. But it wasn't wholly irrational either. Most people felt that, however terrible the crisis was, we could figure out some way of meeting it. They didn't see any sense in tearing up the system, no matter how badly it was working, and trying one that looked good on paper. And they viewed with what turns out to be fully justified suspicion the Russian denial of national self-interest. In short, if we were suckers, most people weren't, and it seems to me that that happy fact deserves to be publicized.

PROPOSAL FOR BOOK-LABELING [3]

After reading "Why You Buy Books That Sell Communism" by Irene Corbally Kuhn (see p. 82 above) . . . and "A Slanted Guide to Library Selections" by Oliver Carlson (see p. 160 below) . . . , I decided to check our public libraries. I asked several ladies to help me. We are not learned people with Ph.D's. We are housewives and mothers. We used as our guide "Review of the Scientific and Cultural Conference for World Peace, arranged by the National Council of the Arts, Sciences and Professions," a report prepared and released by the Committee on Un-American Activities, United States House of Representatives. . . .

A certain amount of our tax money goes toward buying books for these libraries. Authors receive royalties from the sales of their books. Thus every book purchased by our library board contributes to the author's income.

We do not claim that every book listed herein teaches or advocates communism. But we do claim that these books are written by authors who have from one to eighty-five Communist Front affiliations. . . .

[3] From *A Report on Our San Antonio Public Libraries, Communist Front Authors and Their Books Therein*, by Myrtle G. Hance. Mimeographed. Copy furnished by Mrs. J. H. Hance. 230 Overhill Drive. San Antonio, Texas. 1953. p 1-15. Reprinted by permission.

We do not deny any person their constitutional rights. Therefore we do not ask that these books be destroyed, or removed from our public libraries.

However, in honor of our flag, our country, our war dead, our American soldiers fighting in Korea to "contain (?)" communism, as patriotic Americans, citizens and taxpayers, we do request the following:

(1) That each book listed herein, and any books purchased, or donated, be stamped on the inside front cover with a red stamp, large enough to be seen immediately, showing that the author has Communist Front affiliations, and the number of citations. The reader will then realize that in many instances he is reading Communist propaganda.

(2) We request that the books in the main library and all branches be stamped. A group of library employees familiar with the records and index files could easily do this.

(3) We request that a person well informed on pro-Communist books and literature be added to the library board, and that a well-informed committee, such as ours, be allowed to check the index files at intervals and submit their findings of pro-Communist books and literature to the library board, for stamping in the future. . . .

We are certain that there are many more books written by Communist Fronters and pro-Communists in our library that are not listed herein. We do not have their records as yet. As soon as we receive their records, we shall make and release another survey to the public libraries.

The soil of Korea is soaked with the blood of our American soldiers, fighting and dying to prevent communism from engulfing the free world, while we, as taxpayers, are innocently contributing to the support of pro-Communist authors and authors who have Communist citations. . . . To quote Abraham Lincoln, "If this nation is ever destroyed, it will be from within, not from without."

PATTERN FOR RESISTANCE [4]

In San Antonio, Texas, we are at present faced with a two-fold problem concerning censorship. The first aspect of the problem appeared when Mrs. M. Hance and a self-appointed committee of local women put out a bulletin entitled "REaD— READING! a Report on Our San Antonio Public Libraries Communist Front Authors and Their Books Therein, and Dedicated to the UNINFORMED." . . .

The second part of the problem arose when Marshall O. Bell, member of the Texas House of Representatives, introduced a textbook and school library censorship bill. . . .

In order to combat this twofold problem . . . material was collected and presented in a program for the Manuscript Club of San Antonio, Texas. . . .

The definitive portions of Mr. Bell's bill were . . . read, including his request that the constitutional rule concerning the number of readings (three) necessary in the House be suspended since this was an emergency. This was followed by the question, "Do you know how textbooks are chosen in Texas?" (Since all states have rather close screening in the selection of textbooks, and most people are totally unaware of this fact, this can be a very telling point.)

At this point, Benjamin Fine's article, "The Truth About Schoolbook Censorship," in the December 1952 *Parents' Magazine* was read in part. House Report No. 3232, 81st Congress, United States House of Representatives Committee on Lobbying, showing how and why small pressure groups are attempting to influence textbook legislation, is also very apt at this point.

Excerpts from Francis Biddle's book, *The Fear of Freedom*, were also used in this portion of the talk. . . .

The speaker then continued, "Now, let us once again examine the premise presented by the committee chairman and Mr. Bell. Their premise would lead us to believe that both ourselves and our children are in immediate danger of becoming

4 From "Books on Trial in Texas," by Marie Halpenny, freelance writer, chairman of San Antonio committee to fight censorship. *Library Journal*. 78:1179-82. July 1953. Reprinted by permission.

converted to communism through the use of books written by writers whose names appear on lists issued by the Attorney General or the United States House of Representatives Committee on Un-American Activities.

"They declare that they are against communism. So am I, because under communism there is no room for people who disagree with any prevailing line of thought or conduct, as I am doing tonight. At this point I am in complete agreement with the ends stated. But we must know what we are fighting. Saying that we are against communism is like saying we are against sin. The same words may have different meanings to different people. In order to make myself clear, I would like to state my definition of communism. When I think or speak of communism I am thinking or talking about any government or group which operates on the philosophy of fear, fraud and force. This also includes fascism, nazism, and every group, whatever name it may choose, which is a proponent of fear, fraud and force.

"Freedom and democracy cannot coexist with fear—the fear of being different, the fear of error, the fear of being an individual with individual responsibilities. Freedom and democracy cannot exist with fraud. We must remember that fraud of any kind, whether it be shoddy goods or shoddy principles, avoids close examination, while freedom and democracy can not only withstand, but invite, the closest examination in the impartial light of reason. And certainly there is no argument that when force comes to the forefront—whether it be force by arms or force by unconstitutional laws—then the place of freedom and democracy has been usurped. And it is between the philosophies of fear, fraud and force on the one side and democracy and freedom on the other that the battle line is drawn."

At this point the "contaminated" books [previously exhibited] were reintroduced with a word or two about each one. . . .

Some of those not satisfied with the evidence so far presented can usually be depended on at this point to remind you that it is not the books themselves and their contents to which so-and-so objects, but to the writers, since their names appear on certain lists. (This point was emphasized by both the speaker and some of the audience who were unaware that this would be the next question dealt with.)

"Let's examine these lists," continued the speaker. "First of all let's turn to the Attorney General's list. I am not making a case for or against such lists, but since they have been set up as the criteria by which our books should be judged, I feel that we should know something about them. The Attorney General's list is a list of such organizations which for one reason or another the Department of Justice believes to be subversive, and was set up for the purpose of screening government employees.

"Most people, including myself, assume that since this work is done by the Department of Justice, all organizations on the list must have known that they would be named and offered an opportunity to refute any unjust accusations. However, on studying the matter, I found that this did not necessarily hold true.

"Three organizations which had been named on the Attorney General's list went into court to demand a hearing as to why their names should not be stricken from the list. When the case, which the United States Supreme Court decided in favor of these organizations, appeared before the Supreme Court, Mr. Justice Frankfurter, in deciding in their favor, wrote:

Designation has been made without notice, without disclosure of any reasons justifying it, without opportunity to meet the undisclosed evidence or suspicion on which the designation may have been based, and without opportunity to establish affirmatively that the aims and acts of the organization are innocent.

"In this same case Supreme Court Justice Black spoke of these listings as being virtual Bills of Attainder which from the beginning were forbidden to both national and state governments by the Constitution of the United States." (A definition of Bill of Attainder and examples were given, followed by reading Supreme Court Justice Douglas' decision on the case. This Supreme Court Decision is for the October term, Nos. 8, 7 and 71. A very excellent reference.)

It was next pointed out that the United States House of Representatives Committee on Un-American Activities goes even farther afield in naming organizations and individuals, since it includes lists by the Attorney General, lists from Un-American Activities Committees in various states, plus whatever it has compiled in its own investigations. It was also pointed out that these investigations were not a trial, and therefore the witnesses appearing before such committees are not allowed to present evidence to substantiate their answers, or cross-examine witnesses testifying against them. (Excerpts were taken from . . . Francis Biddle's book, *The Fear of Freedom*, illustrating the manner in which such committees link guilt by association.)

By way of comparison, illustrations were given on how such matters were handled by Communists in Russia and Communist-dominated countries. . . .

The attention of the group was drawn to the fact that no totalitarian government, no government of fear, fraud and force, could, as had just been illustrated, allow diversity of opinion to be tolerated privately, much less to be expressed in books or schools, while on the other hand the very life blood of a democracy depends on diversity. Each man in a democracy is allowed an examination and comparison of many ideas rather than having to accept and constantly reiterate stereotyped and orthodox beliefs that have been handed down from someone else. . . .

On May 25 a general meeting was held of those opposing book censorship. They decided to form a permanent organization to fight censorship and similar enroachments on their liberty. Mrs Halpenny was appointed head of this organization. Five committees were named: organization, research, public relations, correspondence, and telephone. . . . The purpose of the organization will be explained to the FBI, which will be asked to send representatives to meetings.

THE PRESIDENT SPEAKS OUT [5]

I forget the author, but it was many years ago, you know, under that famous phrase "the coward dies a thousand deaths

[5] From an address by President Dwight D. Eisenhower, delivered at Dartmouth College commencement, Hanover, New Hampshire, June 14, 1953. Text from *Vital Speeches of the Day*. 19:570-1. July 1, 1953.

but the brave man dies but once." In other words, you can live happily if you have courage, because you are not fearing something that you can't help. You must have the courage to look at all about you with honest eyes. . . .

Look at your country. Here is a country of which we are proud, as you are proud of Dartmouth and all about you and the family to which you belong.

But this country is a long way from perfection—a long way. We have the disgrace of racial discrimination. We have prejudice against people because of their religion. We have crime on the docks. We have not had the courage to uproot these things, although we know they are wrong. . . .

Now, that courage is not going to be satisfied. Your sense of satisfaction is not going to be satisfied if you haven't the courage to look at these things and do your best to help correct them—because that is the contribution you shall make to this beloved country, and your task—each of us as he passes along—should strive to add something.

It isn't enough merely to say, "I love America" and to salute the flag. And to take off your hat as it goes by, and to help sing "The Star-Spangled Banner." Wonderful—we love to do them and our hearts swell with pride because those who went before you worked many years to give to us today this pride and this is a pride in this institution that we think has got great happiness and we know has got great contentment and freedom of soul to many people.

It is not yet done.

Don't join the book burners. Don't think you are going to conceal faults by concealing evidence that they ever existed. Don't be afraid to go into your library and read every book as long as any document does not offend our own ideas of decency. That should be the only censorship.

How will we defeat communism unless we know what it is? What it teaches—why does it have such an appeal for men? Why are so many people swearing allegiance to it? It's almost a religion, albeit one of the nether regions.

Now we have got to fight it with something better. Not try to conceal the thinking of our own people. They are part of America, and even if they think ideas that are contrary to ours, they have a right to have them, a right to record them and a right to have them in places where they are accessible to others. It is unquestioned, or it is not America.

THE BOOK OR THE AUTHOR?[6]

One or more members [of the Jersey City Board of Education] have seen fit to order the removal of four of my books from the library of Jersey City Junior College. It appears that they did so without knowledge of what was in those books. All my books are about literature, or else they try to be literature themselves, and so it is safe to assume that the four in question may be so described. It further appears that the Board of Education was soon made aware of this; but that it decided not to alter its original position, alleging opinions and associations of mine as evidence that in any case I was an undesirable person who should be listened to on no subject whatever. . . .

I received only week before last, from the American Library Association, a copy of its Library Bill of Rights. This document is a welcome sign that groups of Americans are taking their own steps these days to safeguard their existence. I quote its third paragraph: "Censorship of books, urged or practiced by volunteer arbiters of morals or political opinion or by organizations that would establish a coercive concept of Americanism, must be challenged by libraries in maintenance of their responsibility to provide public information and enlightenment through the printed word." The application of these excellent words to the Board of Education's act in removing my books from one of the libraries for which it is responsible may not appear on one count to be perfect, and indeed by my own judgment is not. I hap-

[6] From "If Anybody Wants to Know," address by Mark Van Doren, poet, novelist, critic, professor of English, Columbia University, before Hudson County Chapter of Americans for Democratic Action, Jersey City, New Jersey, February 20, 1951. Published in *American Scholar*. 20, no4:396-405. Autumn 1951. Reprinted by permission.

pen to believe, and I have often said, that the right of school authorities to select the books their students shall read is not to be infringed. But on another count the application is clear. The Jersey City Board of Education, after conceding that my books are unobjectionable, still call their author objectionable—do so publicly—and still presume to protect the students of at least one college from contact with his mind.

They do this to me, it might appear, because they disagree with some of my opinions and disapprove of some of my associations. I say "it might appear," for I am not at all certain that they know any more about my opinions than they do about my books; though it is clear that they jump to conclusions, and want others to do so, from the associations they list and allege. I do not propose to challenge their list, though to the best of my knowledge it is sometimes erroneous, and at other times, if not erroneous, misleading. . . .

The one thing the Board did not do—indeed, by saying that the case was "closed" it showed it did not want to do it—was to discover what my opinions actually were and are, to consider their truth or untruth, and if they seemed untrue, to refute them by fair means. . . . If I have ever been wrong in anything I publicly said or joined others in saying, I deserve to be proved wrong and in fact should welcome it. . . . This, I take it, is the process of civilization. By the same token it is not, I take it, the process of civilization to say of someone with whom you disagree either that he is your personal enemy—which does not follow at all—or that he is the enemy of his country and of civilization itself. To be called irrelevant and erroneous names in an argument is not agreeable, and it does not settle the argument. It is a dangerous method even for those who use it, since it can be turned against them. If I am your enemy, then you are mine, and I may be forced to question your motives for thinking and saying what you do. . . .

My faith in the American people and their government—even though some members of that government have shown signs of panic—is still so great that I say this here and now: Whenever I shall be asked my opinion on any crucial matter, and when I have an opinion that I feel deeply, I will express it and join others in expressing it; and I will never bring pressure to bear, by prejudicial publicity, on anybody who disagrees with me, though I will argue with him as capably as I can, and if he is more capable, or proves that he is better informed, I will change my mind and admit that I have done so.

This for me is the essence of Americanism. But there seem to be Americans (I do not know how many) who are so bent upon having everybody agree with them (I don't know exactly about what) that they take another line. If they cannot have agreement in fact, they want it in the form of silence. Nobody must say anything or belong to anything. For the penalty, if he does, is that they will accuse him of supporting a foreign force. That force, it goes without saying, is communism; or it is Russia, which gives communism today whatever force it has. But there is an astonishing similarity between the two dogmatisms. In Russia also there is no third alternative to agreement or silence. I still believe with all my heart that for us this third alternative exists—and not only exists, but is necessary to our survival. I still maintain that it is obligatory for all Americans to speak their minds on matters of common importance, with the understanding that the proper penalty for their being wrong, if they are wrong, is that someone prove them so. . . .

Many Americans are afraid today. And if enough more become so, we shall have lost our freedom. Freedom and courage come and go together, like liberty and argument. . . . The last thing we should fear is communism itself, which some Americans denounce in one breath as contemptible and then in the next breath honor by trembling before its supposed power. It would have no power if they believed in themselves. It could not dominate them if they knew it couldn't. An American poet—poets sometimes do speak of serious matters—recently published his opinion that we as a people are already dominated by communism. He meant, by fear of communism, and by an obsession with it that prevents us from thinking of any other subject. I do not like to think that this is true. There is still time, I trust, for us to come back to the business of being ourselves, and of making our own life as free and strong as men can make it. . . .

The shortest way to weaken ourselves for any struggle we may have with Russia is to throw away the one imperishable strength we have, our faith in individual liberty and dignity, and our faith that the life of any democratic society is measured by the number of its members who believe it to be necessary, for the common good and for their own, that they think as well as they are able, and speak as sensibly as they can. . . .

I am opposed to communism, both as a theory and in the form it now takes before the world; but I should like to distinguish between my opposition to it and that of certain anti-Communists who think they need be nothing else. The good life is both negative and positive; it is against what would hurt it, but at the same time that it makes itself safe it considers what it wants to be safe for, and what it could build if it were free. . . .

Communists can say what they do not mean, for purposes of their own; but we must mean, for no purpose beyond our integrity, whatever we say. And we must not stop talking. We may or may not arrive at the truth; but we shall utterly fail if we desist from the attempt.

UNITED STATES LIBRARIES ABROAD

EDITOR'S INTRODUCTION

Nowhere has the search for subversive authors been more vigorously pursued than in the United States Information libraries in other countries. Collections in these libraries have been a prime target of Senator Joseph R. McCarthy's investigators and supporters. Directives to these libraries, frequently revised under pressure from this group of critics, and conflicting interpretation of the directives have tended to confuse rather than to clarify the issue.

A review of the conflict over information library policies is contributed to this section by a newspaper librarian who has followed the situation closely in Washington. Next come quotations from the testimony of a former Communist editor, pointing up that Communist efforts to invade the book field do present a serious problem to be met in selecting books to represent American thought to alien readers.

A liberal editor gives the results of his survey of what patrons want from these libraries and why. Finally, a Washington correspondent clarifies the objectives of the United States Information Service in establishing libraries to give our friends abroad a true picture of our country.

U.S. LIBRARIES DISPUTE [1]

The recent furor over the books in the overseas libraries began February 18, 1953, when the Subcommittee on Investigations of the Senate Committee on Government Operations questioned the novelist Howard Fast. The questioning by Senator Mc-

[1] From "U. S. Libraries," by Salvatore D. Nerboso, librarian, New York *Times* Washington Bureau. *Library Journal.* 79:20-5. January 1, 1954. Reprinted by permission.

Carthy, chairman of the subcommittee, and Senator Mundt indicated that a recently issued State Department directive on
"controversial authors" rather than Howard Fast was the real
target. . . .

Rather than advocating the indiscriminate use of materials
by Communists, as the questioning of the subcommittee implied,
the directive set forth a rather moderate policy and contained
specific criteria:

> In the selection of materials . . . it should be possible as a
> general rule, to draw upon the great body of resources available
> produced by persons whose ideological position is unquestioned. Ad-
> mitting, however, that usefulness to IIA [the International Information
> Administration] is the basic consideration governing inclusion of any
> materials in IIA collections, there are times when items produced by
> ideologically questionable persons may be advisable. In view of the
> great resources available to IIA the latter action would necessarily be
> the exception. The criteria governing that exceptional action are the
> following:
>
> 1. Content of the product, not authorship, will be the primary
> criterion. This means that other factors are to be considered.
>
> 2. Materials produced by a person whose ideologies and views are
> questionable or controversial will not be used unless:
>
> (a) the material supports importantly (not incidentally) a
> specific IIA objective; and the converse, that is, none of the content
> is detrimental to the objectives of the United States Government.
>
> (b) the material is substantially better than other material available
> for the purpose, that is, support of a specific objective of IIA.
>
> 3. The effectiveness of the material judged as promoting im-
> portantly a specific IIA objective, has been weighed against the possible
> harm resulting from enhanced prestige the controversial producer may
> acquire by virtue of the inclusion of his product in IIA operations.
> The balance must be clearly and strongly in favor of the effectiveness
> of the material.

The senators were somewhat mollified when Mr. Connors
[W. Bradley Connors, Assistant Administrator for Policy and
Plans for the IIA] stated that the February 3 directive had been
canceled and a memorandum had been issued that "no materials by any controversial persons, Communists, fellow travelers,
et cetera, will be used under any circumstances in any IIA
media." . . .

This memorandum opened a Pandora's box of confusion, which required the individual librarian at an overseas post to translate "et cetera," to say nothing of the other parts of the directive, into policy direction for day-by-day operations. . . .

From this time until July 8 the State Department issued ten directives or supplementary instructions on the subject of books in the overseas libraries. . . . On March 17 a directive was issued stating that books written by Communists were not to be allowed in the overseas libraries, and that authors who followed the Communist line or belonged to front organizations were to be considered Communists for the purposes of these instructions. . . . On April 23, the overseas libraries were directed to remove works of authors who had refused to testify, under the protection of the Fifth Amendment, regarding alleged Communist affiliations. In a directive dated May 13 . . . librarians were directed to remove the works of authors who had refused to testify before that [McCarthy] committee regarding Communist connections. Two days later the State Department cautioned that books removed were to be stored, not burned. . . .

The practical difficulties . . . of a librarian in India in determining who had appeared before various congressional committees and refused to testify . . . would have made the administrative problem impossible even if the policy directives had been clear and consistent. . . .

The controversy entered another phase when on June 14 President Eisenhower made a speech at Dartmouth College . . . [in which he] said: "Don't join the book burners. Don't think you are going to conceal faults by concealing evidence that they ever existed." . . .

The following day Secretary of State Dulles revealed that eleven books had literally been burned as a result of the confusion and fear caused by the directives. . . .

In the next presidential press conference, June 17, the lines blurred again. . . . The President refused to state whether his [Dartmouth] speech was critical of the McCarthy school of thought, on the grounds that he never talked personalities. . . .

In a letter dated June 24 to Robert B. Downs, President of the American Library Association, President Eisenhower seemed to return more to his position in the Dartmouth speech. [That letter is quoted in the final section of this volume—Ed.]

In identical letters dated June 25 [sent to two senators] . . . Secretary of State Dulles [said]:

> On February 24, 1953, with the President's approval, I appointed Dr. Robert L. Johnson to become Director of the International Information Administration, and on March 17, 1953, I advised him that I did not think that the IIA should make the works of Communist authors a part of its foreign libraries or subscribe to periodicals which are receptive to international Communist propaganda. My memorandum to Dr. Johnson concluded, "If you find these ideas acceptable, I must rely on you to translate them into what is an appropriate and practicable 'working level' directive." I have not since personally intervened in this matter.

In the course of the press conference [the same day] neither Dr. Johnson nor his assistant appeared able to define the criteria for accepting or rejecting a "controversial" author or work. . . .

The State Department on June 26 sent out a directive stating that no additional books were to be removed purely on the basis of authorship without consideration of content, except in the case of authors specifically named in instructions. A directive issued on June 30 ordered that books removed on the basis of authorship alone and without specific instruction were to be returned to the shelves. . . .

On July 6 Dr. Robert L. Johnson, Director of the International Information Administration, announced he would soon resign because of poor health. . . . Two days later the long-awaited Policy Statement on the Government's Book and Library Policy was presented to the press by Dr. Johnson. . . . The core of the policy is found in the following:

> We must begin with the content of a book. We must examine its special usefulness in terms of our overseas needs. An appraisal of this usefulness cannot disregard the reputation or standing of the author.
>
> It is conceivable that the special purpose character of our libraries may require in special cases the inclusion of books by Communists or

Communist sympathizers if such authors may have written something which affirmatively serves the ends of democracy. There is no objection to the inclusion of such books so long as the purpose is clear.

"Controversial" books are of course acceptable and indeed essential if by controversy we mean honest differences of opinion honestly expressed.

The policy statement of July 8 is now in effect. A comparison will show that it sets forth essentially the same policy as the February 3 directive that content and usefulness toward the accomplishment of program objectives will be the criteria for book selection. . . .

The basic elements of the situation are today exactly as they were in February. . . . The controversy has done severe and perhaps irreparable damage to the prestige of the United States and the information program. . . . Dr. Johnson's successor [Theodore C. Streibert] will need deep wisdom, extraordinary courage, the backing of President Eisenhower, and the support of the American people to furnish the type of leadership that will make itself felt at the lowest operating level and carry forward the information program under the policy directive of July 8. Perhaps it is not too late to restore the United States to its traditional position as the symbol of freedom of thought and expression.

RED BOOKS IN U.S. LIBRARIES [2]

Mr. COHN [Roy M. Cohn, chief counsel of committee]: Now, Professor Budenz, I might ask you this: During the period of time you were in the Communist party and served on its commissions and held high office in it, did you acquire any knowledge concerning the use to which the Communist party put those of its members who were authors of books?

Mr. BUDENZ: Yes. The Communists consider books a very vital part of psychological warfare, as we now call it. They

[2] From testimony of Louis F. Budenz, former managing editor of the *Daily Worker*, now a professor at Fordham University, March 25, 1953. In transcript of hearings before Permanent Subcommittee on Investigations of the Senate Committee on Government Operations. 83d Congress, 1st Session. Superintendent of Documents, Washington 25, D.C. 1953. Part 1, p41-59.

understand that if they can poison the wells of public opinion by any means, and they seek to infiltrate every channel of public-opinion-making, they can gain great headway, making people in the country they wish to undermine think as the Kremlin wants them to think.

Now, books are a very important weapon in this campaign. They need not necessarily always be Communist in character, because the prestige of the author also counts. If an author, for example, is put in a high school library in the United States, we will say, the Communists count on his name becoming an authority among the students. Therefore, when he says that he will not fight the Communist Chinese if ordered by the United States Government, that has its effect upon those pupils and students who have looked up to him as an authority.

Mr. COHN. Did the Communist party, to your knowledge, attempt to exercise any control over those of its members who were authors of books?

Mr. BUDENZ: Definitely. They exercised a very strict control over those authors. As a matter of fact, they keep someone constantly—that is, a functionary, as they call them—in touch with these people.

Mr. COHN: And what were the duties of that functionary?

Mr. BUDENZ: That functionary is to see that this person, under directives of the party, follows out the Communist line in accordance with the particular area or field in which he is operating. He may be a fiction writer. There he will have to introduce, when he can, Marxism-Leninism, but there are certain aspects of writing where you can't do that, really. But in that case he will have to be a member of a Communist front, lend himself to Communist causes, or give large sums of money to the Communist party.

Mr. COHN: Did you ever hear any discussion within the Communist party concerning the desirability of placing books in places under the sponsorship of the United States Government?

Mr. BUDENZ: Yes; I did. I don't recall definite directives on that matter, but I know the whole question of placing books, by the Government, in the schools, abroad, and at home, was discussed. And not only discussed but was considered an important item in Communist activity. . . .

The CHAIRMAN [Senator Joseph R. McCarthy]: Mr. Budenz, can you think of any reason why those in the Information Service would purchase the books of well-known Communists, men like Browder and Foster, and others, and place them throughout the world in our libraries, in order to, as they say, fight communism?

Mr. BUDENZ: No; that is totally unknown to me, as to how this could come about, save that there was the advice of some concealed Communist at work in this respect. I can't conceive of it otherwise.

The CHAIRMAN: In other words, you feel that that must have been the work of a Communist; otherwise it would not have been done?

Mr. BUDENZ: That is right; a concealed Communist must have at least given advice. I don't say that the administrative officer in charge was such, or anyone like that, but certainly someone along the line was a concealed Communist, to give advice of that character. None of these books would be there. I don't care what their number is. Because they openly advocate, in many instances, the overthrow of the government of the United States, or lend their aid to that cause, to Marxism-Leninism, which is, in its very heart, the violent overthrow of the government of the United States on behalf of the Soviet dictatorship. . . .

Senator [Stuart] SYMINGTON: We have had several, if not quite a few, witnesses who have been willing to state that they were not Communists now, but refused to answer as to whether or not they had been Communists, say, before 1950. . . . Do you think that as a group they are sincere in having left the Communist party?

Mr. BUDENZ: I would say the very fact that they refused to testify as to whether or not they were members of the Communist party in 1950 indicates that they made an arrangement with the Communist party for technical resignation. . . .

Senator [John L.] McCLELLAN: In other words, if they publish books that are completely, in their terms and provisions, derogatory to the American system and favorable to the system that prevails in Russia, that is a very reliable test of whether they are really Communists or Communist sympathizers, and whether they are real loyal Americans?

Mr. BUDENZ: Most decidedly, because that is a very important factor, as I have stated, in what we now call psychological warfare on the part of Soviet Russia. It has understood, shrewdly, for years, that it must penetrate in one way or another all policy-making bodies in order to mold the minds of the people, in this country or that, which they wish to undermine, according to the desires of the Kremlin.

Senator McCLELLAN: These media of books and documents that are made available in public libraries are sources of propaganda that the Communists in Russia regard highly as being effective?

Mr. BUDENZ: That is correct.

Senator McCLELLAN: And we use taxpayers' money to supply these books to libraries supported and maintained by this Government, when they are actually aiding the enemy in so doing, are we not?

Mr. BUDENZ: Yes, sir, Senator. . . .

Senator McCLELLAN: Well, the very fact that we buy them with taxpayers' money and place them in a library maintained by the Government lends credence to their value.

Mr. BUDENZ: Yes. Well, I would say, then, that this is a method of breeding communism throughout the world.

Senator McCLELLAN: It is certainly not a weapon to fight communism, is it?

Mr. BUDENZ: It is not. It is breeding communism. It is encouraging communism. I think we cannot escape that conclusion.

Senator SYMINGTON: Professor, you once were a Communist, and then you renounced that faith. Have you ever written any books since you did renounce it?

Mr. BUDENZ: Yes, I have. . . .

Senator SYMINGTON: Do you happen to know whether the renunciation as you expressed it in those books . . . has been used by our Government in the libraries?

Mr. BUDENZ: . . . I do not know, one way or another.

The CHAIRMAN: Mr. Budenz, there has been a tremendous hue and cry raised since the Jenner committee has commenced to expose Communist teachers and professors. They cry that they are impairing academic freedom.

As a former top man of the Communist party, would you say that there is any freedom of thought, any freedom of action, on the part of those Communist teachers?

Mr. BUDENZ: The only way to defend academic freedom is to get rid of the Communists in all our educational systems. Because they will destroy academic freedom immediately by their activities, and, secondly, in the long run, if they get control of the education system. The Communist goes into the school system under directives. As a matter of fact, there are many printed documents to that effect issued by the Communist party. He goes under printed directives. He must follow the Communist party line. He is not supposed to expose himself, incidentally, Senator, and he doesn't have to teach communism openly in the classroom, if that will cause him to be expelled. But he does it covertly, indirectly, subtly. And in that way he finds out those pupils who are most susceptible and cultivates them personally, finds out those colleagues on the teaching staff who are most susceptible and cultivates them personally. . . .

The CHAIRMAN: Would you care to explain to us why the Communist party considered it so important to infiltrate the newspapers and radio, and what the function of the members in the radio and newspapers happened to be?

Mr. BUDENZ: The Communist party endeavors to infiltrate every agency of public opinion, and they endeavor particularly to infiltrate bottlenecks of public opinion. They therefore considered any agency that would be able to affect the minds of others of importance. And their infiltration was on that basis. As a matter of fact, they considered the newspaper field so important that for a while they had control of the American Newspaper Guild. Fortunately, that condition has ceased, and they have been defeated there. But that, in the beginning, was the situation. And it was due to their interest in affecting agencies of public opinion. . . .

Mr. COHN: Now, what was the policy of the Communist party insofar as use of these books in things like information centers throughout the world was concerned, from your experience, under the sponsorship of the State Department?

Mr. BUDENZ: Perhaps I can illustrate this best by the use of the books within the United States, which I helped to direct, and that is the placing of books in the libraries of our high schools and colleges. That was a specific responsibility for the purpose of, first, getting out the ideas of the authors to the students, making them required reading whenever possible, and then, secondly, using the prestige of the author so that when he engaged in any activity such as a pro-Communist cause, these people who had read his book would look up to him as an authority. We can see that in a somewhat similar manner this could be the use of this abroad.

WHY PATRONS USE U.S. INFORMATION LIBRARIES [3]

The real story [of the United States Information Service libraries abroad] is one in which Americans can take justifiable pride. Certainly I know how good I felt when I saw, day after day, the tangible evidence of the effectiveness of our program.

In Hiroshima, for example, the American library had become something of a community center of ideas. There were public forums and lectures with open stacks as background. The very climate seemed attuned to reconditioning, and our books were making a substantial contribution.

In Colombo, Ceylon, the only complaint I heard from local people was that the library wasn't large enough. In Calcutta I found the American library . . . one of the busiest places in the city. In New Delhi, I met educators who described the library as an indispensable adjunct to the local universities. In Cairo I

[3] From "Open the Books," editorial by Norman Cousins, editor, *Saturday Review*. *Saturday Review*. 36:30-1. July 11, 1953. Reprinted by permission.

met agricultural students who acknowledged their great debt to American agricultural research, as reported in books and professional journals available at the local American library . . . .

In Heidelberg and a half dozen other German cities I found people whose ideas about our country and our people were being shaped by their freedom to read about us, rather than by the stereotypes of hostile propaganda. The same was true in Rome, Athens, and Paris.

The big thing we had done in all these places, of course, was to say in effect: "This library is not large, but it is fairly representative of the cross-section of American thought. These are the books we ourselves read. The emphasis is on nonfiction, but that is because of the large number of requests we have for books that fill the large gap of the war years in the technical and scientific fields, and because these books are directly useful in improving farms, in setting up health and sanitation projects, and in raising the living standards of people. The periodicals, too, represent a cross-section of what Americans read. They are intended for your information and enjoyment.

"Whether with respect to books or magazines, there has been no attempt to 'censor' your reading or to try to tailor your thoughts. Our libraries are intended as showcases of American freedoms, of which the freedom to read and think is the most important. If your ideas of America are clearer because of what you read here, if your local problems are closer to solutions because of the aid you find here, then these libraries will have served their purpose and the American people will feel fully rewarded for the effort and money expended in this work."

But in recent weeks we have stopped saying this. Instead we have said, in effect: "Many of the American men and women who operate these libraries are under suspicion of disloyalty by members of Congress. We cannot make a presumption of innocence in their favor. Not long ago we made such a presumption in the case of a highly placed official and we later learned we were wrong. And now we are carefully scrutinizing all personnel records.

"What is worse, there are books by Communists on the bookshelves of our libraries. These books must be removed. There is no reason why American taxpayers should buy books by those who would destroy this nation. Moreover, we have such little confidence in your intelligence, in your ability to weigh all the evidence on the basis of everything we have to offer, that certain books must be kept from you. In some cases we will even set a match to them.

"In any event, the American people are not entirely pleased with the way this library program has been going, and we intend to bring it into line. Incidentally, we are going to remove books by American authors who are in no way identified with communism. They have written books that are controversial and so forth, and the executive branch of government would rather not be involved in unnecessary controversy at this time." . . .

The Asian newspapers have given prominence to the official American admission that some books have actually been burned in our libraries abroad. Do we have any right to suppose that the news of our stumbling and fumbling over books does not do severe damage to the American cause throughout the world? What do we do about the charge that a nation that became great because of the free flow of ideas has itself become frightened of ideas? And if we take the position that we don't care a fig what the rest of the world thinks, what right do we have operating a foreign information and library service in the first place? The fact is that our standing in the world today is important: in fact, our security depends as much upon good will as upon any other effort we are making. That is why it is so ironic that through our own hideous ineptness we have done damage to ourselves far beyond anything done against us by the Soviet propaganda machine.

It is no reply to this merely to say that the American people have a right to protect themselves against the Communist conspiracy, and that they are under no obligation to support the works of authors who are identified with this conspiracy. This is a poor reply for two reasons. First, we must make a distinction between ordering books and removing books. There is considerable latitude in placing a book on the shelves, but an altogether different problem is involved in removing it once it gets there. Buying a book involves choice. Removing it, banning it, or burning it is an entirely different proposition. What is involved in this latter case is an overt act against the world of ideas. It makes pygmies of the burners and martyrs of the books and their authors.

There is a second reason why it is not enough to say that Americans are justified in removing books because the authors are part of a Communist conspiracy. This reason has already been demonstrated. Simply, it is this: we have proved we can't tell the difference between a Communist and a democrat. The order against books is an indiscriminate one. It is directed against books that are "Communist, controversial, and so forth." What is the distinguishing characteristic of a free society if not controversy? No government in history has known enough to be able to prescribe a diet of ideas for its people. And ideas to be any good must be able to survive the heat of controversy. Yet we have the astonishing spectacle of the American government placing a ban on books that are controversial as being synonymous with subversion.

PURPOSE OF LIBRARIES ABROAD [4]

The State Department, under heavy attack for its so-called "book-burning" or book-banning policies, has begun to show some concern over what its highest officials believe is a misunderstanding of its overseas information task.

These quarters not only deny that a threat to basic academic freedom is inherent in excluding certain books or authors from United States information centers abroad, but also point out that the law establishing those centers specifically limited the type and scope of information that should be available to them.

The State Department has been charged with "confusion" in the administration of policy directives barring the use of books

4 From "Dulles' Aides Cite 'Mission' on Books," by Walter H. Waggoner, New York *Times* Washington correspondent. New York *Times*. p 16. July 1, 1953. Reprinted by permission.

by Communists, pro-Communists or certain "controversial figures," and the department has acknowledged some confusion.

It is the opinion of some officials whose views are shared by John Foster Dulles, the Secretary of State, that there also is some public confusion over the role that the State Department is authorized to play.

Critics of the department's directives for weeding out or barring certain books from overseas libraries fail to make the distinction, according to these persons, between a general public or academic library and a library of "special purpose."

The United States overseas libraries received a "special purpose" in the United States Information and Exchange Act of 1948, as follows:

[To] disseminate abroad information about the United States, its people and policies promulgated by the Congress, the President, the Secretary of State and other responsible officials of Government having to do with matters affecting foreign affairs.

This definition, say the authorities responsible for conforming to it, means that the United States' overseas libraries are comparable to medical or engineering libraries. Who, they ask, would argue that detective stories or treaties on communism should be bought or maintained with funds given specifically for medical or engineering scholarships?

It is a matter of some distress to State Department officials, however, that United States information policies that exclude such books, as having no connection with "information about the United States," are regarded as an abridgment of academic freedom.

Secretary Dulles, it is known, believes that there is ample room for disagreement on the application of the law to the contents of overseas libraries, and he personally is in favor of applying the law liberally.

But he also has said, as in his recent letters to Democratic Senators Thomas C. Hennings, Jr., of Missouri and Henry M. Jackson of Washington, that the law that plainly marks the United States information centers as "special purpose" rather than "all purpose" libraries cannot be ignored.

TEXTBOOKS

EDITOR'S INTRODUCTION

Classrooms have been a center for some of the most vigorous controversies in "the struggle for men's minds." This section deals with arguments whether textbooks that present favorably political and economic systems differing from ours are proper material for student minds.

First, the education editor of the New York *Times* describes how textbooks are screened. A critical review of Magruder's *American Government*, long a standard college textbook, illustrates the objections raised by some organizations to criticism of what has been termed "American economic folklore." An act of the Alabama legislature and a news item about the story of Robin Hood show how far this sort of "protection" can go.

An article from an educational journal discusses attempts to bar UNESCO materials from our schools. The case against UNESCO is argued by a contributing editor of a right-wing magazine.

A textbook editor tells of pressures to get certain books used or barred from use in schools. An instructor in historical writing suggests how textbooks may be made "safe" for students. A manifesto issued by a teachers' organization defines the responsibilities of school authorities, teachers, students, parents and civic groups for proper use of classroom materials.

HOW TEXTBOOKS ARE SCREENED [1]

Our school and college textbooks are under fire. In all parts of the land, widespread attacks are being made on books and other classroom materials.

[1] From "The Truth About Schoolbook Censorship," by Benjamin Fine, education editor, New York *Times*. *Parents' Magazine*. 27:46+. December 1952. Reprinted by permission.

Books that have been used for a quarter of a century or more suddenly become "subversive." Books written by men or women who are on so-called "un-American" lists are tossed from the public libraries. Superpatriotic groups, professional agitators, opportunists and those who hate our democratic way of life are smearing scholarly books by below-the-belt name-calling.

What is "subversive"? One critic objects to a text because it praises the Tennessee Valley Authority; another says all economics books favor the New Deal. A third dissenter opposes the use of the term "free public schools" and still another finds a text objectionable because the nation is described as a democracy instead of a republic. . . .

Self-appointed committees are being organized to serve as censors. You and your children are at the mercy of these book vigilantes. Timid school board members or superintendents often run for cover at the least sign of trouble. Call a book subversive, communistic, socialistic or un-American long enough and honest citizens will become confused, too.

Take the case of *American Government*, written thirty-five years ago by Frank Magruder, the most widely used history text for three decades. On July 15, 1949, a review appeared in *Educational Reviewer*, published by the Committee on Education of the Conference of American Small Business Organizations. The reviewer said the book had socialistic and communistic overtones. Passages were taken out of context and distorted to prove how "dangerous" the book was. . . .

Many communities fought back. New Haven's Board of Education appointed a committee of twenty teachers to examine the Magruder text—and gave it a clean bill of health. Council Bluffs [Iowa] recommended that the book be retained. So did Trumbell County [Ohio]. The Florida department of education found the book "objective, accurate and fair." But despite the appraisals by numerous lay and professional committees, Magruder is in for continuing attacks.

Other books are getting the poison-smear treatment, too. . . .

The growth of textbook censorship is causing our leading educators serious concern. School librarians, school principals and superintendents are intimidated. Unwilling to risk their jobs or risk a public controversy, they quietly fold their tents and sneak away from their own ideals. The self-appointed censors often are able to win without firing a shot.

It's not easy when you are on the firing line. School boards are constantly attacked for being "soft" toward communism, for permitting books written by fellow travelers into the classroom. To show the community they are on the job, they start a campaign of their own or follow the lead of the censors. That's the serious problem we now face. The anti-intellectual campaign is a major threat to our democratic society.

In the words of Dr. David K. Berninghausen, for many years chairman of the American Library Association's Committee on Intellectual Freedom, "Copying the Nazis or the Communists in thought control techniques in communications and education is not the way to meet our problem. The antidote to authoritarianism is not some form of American authoritarianism. The antidote is free inquiry."

In a democratic land, all of us have the right to voice our opinion, to criticize a book or anything else, if we so desire. But that criticism should be honest and informed.

You may wonder what assurance you have that the textbooks your child uses are not subversive. Be reassured: hardly a product in the land is so carefully scrutinized as are textbooks. Publishers, editors, textbook selection committees, the teachers who use the books and those who review them, all go over them carefully. Is it reasonable to believe that this cumulative screening would miss subversive, communistic or un-American passages in our textbooks?

Textbook censorship is poisoning America's free spirit, warns Dr. Luther H. Evans, [former] Librarian of Congress. "The experts in vituperation, the sadists of freedom, are abroad in the land, and are having a heyday. We must learn not to fear them. We must show them up for what they are. They are cowards who are unwilling to live the American dream."

Who are these cowards referred to by Dr. Evans? Some are the superpatriots who get excited about books they have never read—but that someone else has charged with being dangerous or subversive. Or they may be organized complainers eager to exploit the present tension for financial or political gains. They may even be professional agitators, who do not like America, and would make it over in their own unwholesome image.

Yet there are many conscientious, honest, decent parents and citizens who are concerned, too. They have heard much wrangling and have seen mud fly. And they are wondering what is happening, and if they can be certain that the charges are based on fact. They are genuinely puzzled.

It should reassure them to know that every community has some form of screening plan. Half the states have uniform textbook commissions, while the rest have local committees that examine all textbooks. Since the books are usually used by all the states, if one community would miss a "subversive" passage, another would catch it soon enough. . . .

Whether the textbooks are screened by state or local committees, the job is unusually thorough. But that is not enough to satisfy the professional agitators, the superpatriots. They see a communist plot on every page.

What can be done about it? New York State is supplying one answer. Recent resolutions by state groups such as the D.A.R, the American Legion and the Federation of Women's Clubs charged that the schools were using textbooks containing subversive, socialistic and un-American material. By action of the State Board of Regents, Commissioner Lewis A. Wilson appointed a three-man commission, consisting of himself as Commissioner of Education, and two lay persons of considerable prestige in the community. Now any person can send whatever complaints he may have to the commission. Established last January, the textbook commission has been widely publicized. Yet at this writing, not a single complaint has been filed.

THE CASE AGAINST MAGRUDER'S
AMERICAN GOVERNMENT [2]

Magruder's *American Government* is an example of the extent to which a textbook, perhaps without intent, may spread

[2] From "Broadcasting Collectivist Propaganda," review by Edna Lonigan, writer on political and economic subjects. *Educational Reviewer*. 1:3. July 15, 1949. Reprinted by permission.

slanted arguments and data issued by governments. In this case, the trouble appears to lie in the uncritical judgment of author and publisher.

In its discussion of "democracy," the book assumes that we have shifted permanently and properly from the American form of "democracy" in which individuals have equal opportunity, to the French form in which people are organized into collective masses, such masses electing governments with absolute power to impose their wills on the individuals. This view of "democracy" leads straight from Rousseau, through Marx, to totalitarianism.

In Chapter XXXVI, "Making Democracy Work," the author says: "By democracy we mean that form of government in which the sovereign power is in the hands of the people collectively." But in America we have a Constitution and Bill of Rights to protect us against the power of the collectivist state. . . . There is nothing in the book to suggest that the American free economy made any contribution to our high employment.

Under "planning," seven lines are given to private industry. Private industry has built power plants, but government builds them "at planned locations." Is the implication that private power companies choose their dam-sites by throwing darts at a map?

The book is not only descriptive, but it proposes remedies for all our difficulties. The remedies follow the pattern of the welfare state, in which all money is collected by, and dispensed by, Washington. Federal medical care is to be "free." Federal aid to education is urged directly and indirectly; likewise Federal housing. . . .

The treatment of race and inequality of income follows the Communist party line. Poor people are always "underprivileged" and "unfortunate."

Italy and Germany were dictatorships, but not the Soviet Union! It educates "all" able students at public expense (except those in forced labor camps). The United States and the Soviet Union are equals fighting for world "leadership." The Russian veto is merely Russia's "safeguard for her minority views on basic matters concerning which the democratic nations would overwhelmingly outvote her." (p714.)   Problems of the Near East should be settled by the United States and the Soviet Union.

An explanation of these fantastic statements and evidence that the author is not consciously propagandizing can be found in the bibliographies. Major reliance is placed on the pamphlet material of the Foreign Policy Association and the Public Affairs Committee, which have been charged again and again with the use of party-line propaganda, and are certainly not fitted for classroom use. Nevertheless the bibliography contains good selections from reputable scholars on both sides. It is heavily overweighted, however, with propaganda material which is popular at the moment, and which enjoys a specious reputation for scholarship only because it has been given a skillful "build-up" by propagandists for the absolute state.

ALABAMA TEXTBOOK LAW [3]

An act relating to schools; to prohibit the use of certain textbooks and writings in public schools, institutions of higher learning, and trade schools.

Be it enacted by the legislature of Alabama:

Section 1. Neither the state textbook committee nor the state board of education or any other public body or official shall consider for adoption or approval, or adopt or approve for use in the public schools or trade schools or institutions of higher learning of this state any textbook or other written instructional material (not including periodical newspapers and magazines nor legal opinions by courts of record) which does not contain a statement by the publisher or author thereof indicating clearly and with particularity that the author of the book or other writing and the author of any book or writings cited therein as parallel or additional reading is or is not a known advocate of communism or Marxist socialism, is or is not a member or ex-

    [3] Text of Act No. 888, H. 644, approved by the Alabama House of Representatives, September 19, 1953. Mimeographed copy provided by American Textbook Publishers Institute. New York. 1953. p 1.

member of the Communist party, and is or is not a member or ex-member of a Communist-front organization (as designated by the United States Congress, or any committee thereof, or the Attorney General of the United States).

Section 2. The use of any book or other writing which is prohibited by this act may be enjoined upon the application of any resident taxpayer.

Section 3. This act shall become effective January 1, 1954. However, this act shall not affect the use of any textbook heretofore adopted or approved for use in this state until one year from the date the act becomes law.

[The Circuit Court of Montgomery County, Alabama, on May 10, 1954, adjudged the above act void, unenforceable, and in violation of the Fourteenth Amendment to the United States Constitution.—Ed.]

IS "ROBIN HOOD" SUBVERSIVE? [4]

The story of "Robin Hood" was under attack today by a member of Indiana's Textbook Commission, who demanded that the tale be removed from school books because it promoted Communist doctrine.

Mrs. Thomas J. White of Indianapolis, Republican member of the State Commission, also demanded banning of all information about the Quaker religion because, she said, it also tended to support communism.

[In Nottingham, England, the present Sheriff of Nottingham said that "Robin Hood was no Communist."]

State Superintendent of Education Wilbur Young said he would reread "Robin Hood" to consider the merits of Mrs. White's charge.

In the meantime, however, the infamous Sheriff of Nottingham will continue to be a villain and not just an injured capitalist to Indianapolis sixth graders.

[4] From "Indiana Censor Fears Little Red Robin Hood," news story by the United Press. New York *Times*. p 1+. November 14, 1953. Reprinted by permission.

Indianapolis' Superintendent of Schools, Dr. H. L. Shibler, said he would not ban present textbook references to Robin Hood, the legendary outlaw and bowman of Sherwood Forest.

Mrs. White charged that "there is a Communist directive in education now to stress the story of Robin Hood.

"They want to stress it because he robbed the rich and gave it to the poor. That's the Communist line. It's just a smearing of law and order and anything that disrupts law and order is their meat." . . .

Mrs. White said references to Quakers should be eliminated from books because: "Quakers don't believe in fighting wars. All the men they can get to believe that they don't need to go to war, the better off the Communists are. It's the same as their crusade for peace—everybody lay down his arms and they'll take over."

Dr. Shibler said he could not find anything subversive about Robin Hood and his band of merrie outlaws, Little John, Friar Tuck, Will Scarlet, and the Maid Marian.

Mrs. White said she often consulted Senator William E. Jenner, Republican of Indiana, about "questionable" authors and persons mentioned in the textbooks.

THE UNESCO CONTROVERSY [5]

You may have heard that UNESCO [the United Nations Educational, Scientific and Cultural Organization] has failed, that it's communistic, and godless—and it's working for world government.

Not one of these charges is true. Not one is supported by facts or documentary evidence. You are, if you believe them, the victim of a well-planned whispering campaign of which the UN is the principal target. The same subversive organizations that have been found to be in the background of the attacks on the public schools are in the vanguard of this chorus of criticism. . . .

[5] From "What About Those Attacks on UNESCO?" by Ruth H. Wagner, associate editor, *Midland Schools*, organ of the Iowa Education Association. *Midland Schools*. 67:12-13+. October 1952. Reprinted by permission.

UNESCO and UN—as well as many other institutions such as the public schools—are much in need of sound, constructive criticism. The writer has not only been one of UNESCO's severest critics . . . [but] has also witnessed at national commission [United States National Commission for UNESCO] meetings some of the most severe criticism ever handed to an organization by its members. . . .

What are the charges [against UNESCO]?

1. UNESCO is accused of publishing the series of booklets entitled *Towards World Understanding* for the purpose of promoting world government.

2. It is said that because of its avowed purpose to promote world government, UNESCO is seeking to destroy patriotism; and that there will be a loss of national sovereignty incurred in the undertaking of world responsibilities.

3. UNESCO is accused of being godless and atheistic.

4. UNESCO is being accused of being "tainted" with communism. . . .

The booklets are reports on a series of international seminars wherein educators from UNESCO's member countries . . . have pooled their knowledge and experience on educating for "world understanding."

These booklets are published so that those who have an interest in the subject matter may have access to full information on the seminars and in the hope that "they will arouse interest and stimulate discussion among teachers in many countries."

An attack on the series *Towards World Understanding* and on UNESCO itself was launched by an organization which calls itself the American Flag Committee in its Newsletter No. 13, issued in October 1951. This four-page multilithed bulletin was titled "A Report to the American People on 'UNESCO.' " The report characterized UNESCO as a "subversive association."

The entire statement is a willful distortion. It bases its case on false interpretation. It twists quotations out of context in attempting to support its claims. . . .

A . . . paragraph attributed to UNESCO by the American Flag Committee is that

The teacher is to begin by eliminating any and all words, phrases, descriptions, pictures, images, classroom material, or teaching methods of a sort causing his pupils to feel or express a particular love for, or loyalty to, the United States of America.

This statement is a complete fabrication. It cannot be found in any one of the booklets in the series.

One of the charges is that UNESCO is "advancing the totally un-American doctrine that the prime function of public education in the United States must be that of capturing the minds of our children, at the earliest possible age, for the cause of political world government."

This, too, is a willful distortion. The fact is that the reports of the seminars discuss neither education in the United States nor world government. What is advocated is international co-operation, international understanding, and loyalty to mankind as a whole. They do advise against the kind of selfish nationalism which leads to the rise of dictators. They do not discuss political world government.

These are the charges of the American Flag Committee, which were included in the *Congressional Record* as an "extension of remarks" on October 18, 1951. Reprints from the *Congressional Record* bearing the seal of the United States of America, have had wide distribution throughout the nation. This is the allegedly factual material which has been the basis of the attack against UNESCO.

The letterhead of the American Flag Committee identifies its headquarters as 876 Granite Street, Philadelphia, Pennsylvania, and its "founder and executive chairman" as W. Henry MacFarland, Jr.

The files and records of the House Committee on Un-American Activities indicate that W. Henry MacFarland, Jr. was director of the Nationalist Action League, whose address was also 876 Granite Street, Philadelphia, Pennsylvania. The Nationalist Action League was cited by former Attorney General Tom Clark as a Fascist organization in a list furnished the

Loyalty Review Board, which was released to the press by the United States Civil Service Commission on April 27, 1949.

Is UNESCO seeking to promote world government or to destroy patriotism?

"There is no real or necessary conflict between a man's deep loyalty to his country and his devotion to the best interests of humanity as a whole," said the *Christian Science Monitor* of July 2 [1952] in an editorial. The editorial points out that educators from fourteen countries, meeting at a UNESCO seminar to study textbooks with regard to their effect on international understanding, agreed that "the teaching of national history should have precedence over both local and world history." It proposes that if American students, grounded first in the principles on which their country was founded, "also see their national history as a glorious chapter in the world-wide struggle of men toward liberty, they will be able to measure up to their full stature as Americans and citizens of the world."

Is UNESCO atheistic and godless?

"Nothing could be further from the truth," says James Marshall, a lawyer who has been a member of the New York Board of Education since 1935. "Religious leaders and God-fearing men of many faiths have participated in the work of UNESCO. Jacques Maritain, the great French philosopher and lay Catholic leader, was one of the men who formulated the UNESCO Constitution and has represented France at UNESCO conferences.

"Reinhold Niebuhr, professor of applied Christianity at the Union Theological Seminary, was a member of the United States Delegation to UNESCO in 1949 and one of the principal speakers there. Monsignor Frederick G. Hochwalt, secretary general of the National Catholic Education Association, was one of the early promoters of UNESCO and a United States delegate to several of its conferences. In 1946 he delivered the sermon at the mass held in Notre Dame Cathedral for UNESCO. Not long ago he said that 'religion must take the leadership in pointing out that love among men is not only the purpose but the connective tissue of international society,' and he urged all religious people to support UNESCO and make their influence felt in its program."

Is UNESCO tainted with communism?

Soviet Russia is not and never has been a member of UNESCO. [The Soviet Union joined UNESCO in April 1954—Ed.]. Three satellite nations belong—Poland, Czechoslovakia and Hungary—but since their communization they have played little part in the UNESCO councils. Either they have not been present at UNESCO conferences or they have walked out at each conference. UNESCO refused to seat Communist China in place of Chiang Kai-shek's Nationalist government's representatives. This ought to dispose of all allegations of a Communist taint. . . .

"I think we ought to recognize that some attacks derive from an honest conviction that participation in the UN and UNESCO is not to the best interests of our country," [said Dr. Willard E. Givens in an address at the National Education Association's 1952 Representative Assembly]. "We ought to recognize that in our country, as no doubt in other countries, there are many people who have never accepted the concept of nations working together for peace.

"There are also a growing number of people who believed in the United Nations and UNESCO who have become disillusioned with their programs. We might go even further and say there are valid reasons for some of this disillusionment. . . . I think it is important that we differentiate between honest criticism and the misguided hysteria of 'crack-pots' and other sinister groups who are using attacks on the UN and UNESCO to further their own interests. We must not condemn criticism, nor in examining the critics should we allow ourselves to adopt their tactics.

"The important thing to remember about a W. Henry Mac-Farland, Jr. (or a Gerald L. K. Smith) is not that he is on the Attorney General's list, as happens to be the case, but that the arguments he is using have been persuasive and disturbing to a great many Americans looking for advice, guidance, and help as the cloud of fear envelops them."

CHARGES AGAINST UNESCO [6]

Although UNESCO has staked out activities in eight general fields, most Americans are concerned primarily in what it is trying to do to the American public schools. Here, although the purpose is disguised in high-sounding double-talk, UNESCO is frankly trying to capture the mind of the next generation for "one worldism." With the striking example of how communism has annexed youth in Russia, and now in China, through classroom indoctrination, the UN is skillfully endeavoring to turn the public school into an instrument of internationalist mind-conditioning. . . .

One particular target of UNESCO has been the youngest age group of children. As pointed out in the UNESCO teacher-training booklet, *In the Classroom with Children Under 13 Years of Age:* "These earlier years may be indispensable to the education of children for world citizenship."

A serious concern of the UNESCO school program is to "correct many of the errors of home training." UNESCO points out that "the narrow family spirit of parents may, in fact, not only compromise indirectly, and in some degree, unconsciously, the eventual integration of the child in the human community, but it may also cultivate attitudes running directly counter to the development of international understanding." UNESCO planners see nothing extravagant in the proposal that the child, in the UN-indoctrinated public school, should be taught to despise his parents' social attitudes. . . .

Because so many of the top educators of the country have been tied in with United Nations propaganda and agencies, UNESCO has had things pretty much its own way in the American schools during the last six years. But its "one world" program is now running into an increasing ground swell of popular indignation, which is causing internationalist-minded school heads to take a second look at their position.

[6] From "UNESCO—UN's Brainwashing Apparatus," by Harold Lord Varney, contributing editor, *American Mercury*. *American Mercury*. 78:3-9. February 1954. Reprinted by permission.

Other projects of UNESCO are similarly pointed toward American mind-control. Perhaps the most insolent undertaking is the plan to rewrite world history, in the spirit of internationalism.

Late in 1952, it was announced with fanfare that UNESCO had allocated $600,000 to underwrite a new world history, in six volumes, which should eliminate "bias." One thousand scholars, working for five years, were to be recruited in this task. . . .

Aside from the fact that the proposal to write an official version of human history is a project that smacks unpleasantly of the Kremlin, the whole undertaking is a stern reminder to Americans of the authoritarian spirit which lurks under the facade of the internationalists. . . .

UNESCO promulgated an official "Statement on Race" on July 18, 1950, which came out flatly for miscegenation. "No convincing evidence has been adduced," said the statement, "that race mixture of itself produces biological bad effects. There is, therefore, no biological justification for prohibiting intermarriage between persons of different ethnic groups." . . .

Whatever may be the ultimate scientific decision in the raging controversy on race divergencies, the fact remains that a formidable body of scientific world opinion rejects the Huxley-Boas-Frazier thesis of race identity. It is difficult to escape the conclusion that, in placing its official stamp on this disputed theory, UNESCO is trying to twist science to its purposes. In doing so it is committing a crime against intellectual integrity that even Hitler and Stalin would have envied. . . .

UNESCO is the nearest thing to a "managed" world culture that has emerged in this confused postwar world. Its skillful admixture of acceptable and noncontroversial projects with its coercive programs has disarmed many of its natural critics. The fact that some sincere and deserving men and women have penetrated its staff does not explain away the fact that its high command, since the beginning, has been steered by grim-minded men who are out to submerge American nationalism under a superworld administration.

TEXTBOOK PRESSURES [7]

It should be said at the start that the textbook business in America today is on the whole an illustrious example of the benefits and advantages of the private enterprise system. It would be a sorry day for the youth of America if textbook publishing ever came into the political picture as a result of government management. There is too much politics associated with it now.

→ Textbook publishers spend thousands upon thousands of dollars to issue the best books that can be written and produced. They secure the most skillful artists, they make constant study of reading hygiene, they keep abreast of the latest educational methods. And they would like to be educators; they would like to guide American youth along sound educational paths. Instead, most of them are, frankly, industrialists and manufacturers who too often have to twist their product into several patterns to cater to the fears, prejudices, suspicions, fads and animosities of their market.

How can this be? asks the American parent.

First, textbooks are definitely slanted to the section of the country in which they are to be sold. If, for example, that most attractive history book that your high-school son or daughter brings home sells widely in a section of the country which is sensitive to racial issues or to its participation in the Civil War, that textbook almost inevitably tells half truths, whitewashes facts, or suppresses history completely. The Ku Klux Klan may be elevated to almost virtuous heights or at least satisfactorily accounted for; the slavery issue is soft-pedaled; the textbook cannot contain a picture of a Negro and a white person together, unless the Negro is obviously a servant or laborer. The achievements of the Negro may be listed to be sure, but their struggles to obtain privileges which are guaranteed to them in a democracy are carefully sidestepped. Orientals and Latin American peoples are played down in other sections of the country.

[7] From "America's Schoolbook Scandal," by Clara Stilwell, pseudonym of a textbook editor. *Christian Herald.* p 17-18+. September 1950. Reprinted by permission.

In fairness it must be said, too, that minority groups (usually their leaders only, not the people as a whole) are often super-sensitive to historical fact or some innocent reference to their race. For example, a few years ago in the city of Washington, D.C., an elementary textbook in reading was adopted for city-wide use. A member of the school department, a Negro, dis-covered an illustration in the book showing a small girl holding a Negro mammy doll. The publisher was thereupon required to recall many hundreds of copies of the book, tear out the offend-ing picture, and rebind. Such colossal waste, which the public pays for, and such supersensitive attitudes, tear down rather than build interracial friendship. It is an example—though in this case a relatively harmless one, from the educational point of view —of what publishers are up against.

But frequently these pressure groups exercise a much more harmful influence. Let us suppose that a social science text is offered for sale in a city or section where labor is in ill-repute. The book is scrutinized by a so-called "textbook committee," or by the local school board. It passes muster except for the chapter on industrial relations. That chapter presents too rosy a picture. The CIO or the AFL, these leaders feel, are trouble-makers; they bring about strikes that cripple and discredit the free enter-prise system. So either the text is thrown out of consideration altogether, or the publisher is asked to have the offending section deleted or rewritten.

Textbooks are likewise a handy football for the big-fisted "All-American" politician. One of the ablest, most loyal and intelligent teachers of American history, David Saville Muzzey, has written history books for high schools for many years. His *The Story of Our Country* was adopted for use in the high schools of Chicago a few years back. But because Professor Muzzey dared to suggest that there have been inevitably a few black spots on our country's record, that there are policies and places where we can make America a greater and finer nation, "Big Bill" Thompson [mayor of Chicago from 1915 to 1923 and 1927 to 1937] brought his influence to bear and got the book thrown out of the Chicago schools. When something like that happens, the substituted textbook that is placed in the hands of your children may give an incomplete picture of some very important aspects of American life and history.

Again, as frequently happens, an organization or individual detects some "un-American" sentiment in a book. Such a charge is the special delight of a schoolboard member trying to rake up some startling charges with which to enliven his election campaign. Now, no intelligent person wants to debunk American heroes and American traditions or to disillusion American school children as to the greatness of their country or the priceless heritage that is theirs. But by "un-American" these vocal minority groups seem to mean any slight suggestion that our country was ever in the wrong or that there is anything about it that could be improved. . . .

It is of course no secret that there are leftist groups who would if they could smear America and subtly indoctrinate our children with the perversions of communism or some other "ism" foreign to our way of life. General Bradley, not noted for speaking off the top of his mind, recently warned, "This country harbors a lot of people teaching a different ideology, a different way of government, who work undercover in every community. Some of the things being taught our kids in school are contrary to our way of thinking."

The General went on to tell of four counties near Youngstown, Ohio, in which 103 local industries are underwriting textbooks to teach Americanism, free enterprise and democracy. I would take issue with his enthusiasm at that point. The established textbook publishing houses, themselves operating under the free enterprise system, have access to the brains and possess the know-how to do the job adequately, admirably and with a national rather than local viewpoint—if enough citizens determine to keep pressure groups both of left and extreme right off their necks. . . .

So much for content. There are in addition other serious and ominous facts which parents should know and do something about. How are your children's textbooks purchased? . . . Sometimes, as they should always be, they are selected by the teachers who will use them and who are the best judges of their merits. Too often, they are bought through politics, and sometimes by worse methods. . . .

Politics gets in its . . . hand most frequently in state adoptions. A "state adoption" means that one textbook in a subject, or possibly two, is selected for use by all the schools in the entire state. . . . Such state adoptions are juicy plums. They mean a whale of a lot of business, or none at all, and the competition is consequently terrific. Because of the potential possibilities for corruption, and because the classroom teacher has little to say about the books chosen, such state adoptions should be outlawed. . . .

It is generally recognized that large sales in any business are ordinarily made through a process of "cultivation." That is legitimate salesmanship. Bookmen cultivate their customers, too, and often are exceedingly helpful to them in educational service. But textbooks should not be bought and sold on the same basis as are pie pans.

HOW TO MAKE TEXTBOOKS "SAFE" [8]

Efforts to ban textbooks, particularly those in the social sciences, are not infrequent on the American scene. They are initiated by persistent pressure groups, the most vocal of which are watchdogs of 100 per cent Americanism (generally interpreted as demanding unstinting support of laissez-faire economics), certain racial and religious groups, and some business organizations. All these watchdogs are amazingly, if understandably, sensitive to any opinion that the author of a textbook might express, especially to what he might say or fail to say about them. They are, moreover, trigger-quick about demanding direct action, in the form of a ban, against the books they disapprove of. . . .

[8] From "What to Do About 'Dangerous' Textbooks," by Edward N. Saveth, instructor in historical writing and American intellectual history, New School for Social Research, New York. *Commentary*. 13:99-106. February 1952. Reprinted by permission.

In all this fuss about textbooks, two quite distinct questions are involved. The first is: How bad are the textbooks? The second: If they are bad, what is the best way of seeing that they become better?

Sometimes textbooks are written by leading men in a particular field; more often they are written by run-of-the-mill educators with no little assistance from the editorial office of the publisher, some years after the work of the leading men has seeped down through the classrooms of the teachers' colleges. In consequence of the time lag, and because textbooks long obsolescent continue to be used, such books reflect the expert thinking of ten or twenty years ago. . . . And if we consider the way economists were talking about the American economy fifteen years ago—in the middle of the wreckage of the 1929 crisis, when the unaided efforts of the capitalists only succeeded in deepening the depression, when businessmen cried out for government loans, government regulation and government planning, when so many people saw in an unregulated economic system the cause of the depression—it is easy to see why many textbooks emphasize the weaknesses of a free economy, the importance of planning, and the value of governmental control. . . .

Admittedly, any view on economics or immigration or anything else is not immune to criticism simply by virtue of having found the refuge of a textbook; admittedly textbooks cannot be above the judgment of the community; admittedly the more criticism we have, the better. . . . But what should be the process of this criticism? How can the community act so as really to improve textbooks without wrecking its school system? . . .

The principal method has been that of professional criticism —criticism by educators and scholars within the field, themselves disturbed at the divergence between the most authoritative findings of research and the views presented in textbooks. Most scholars today will freely concede that there is a good deal wrong with our textbooks. . . .

What improvement there has been in the American textbook in the past quarter century has been primarily in response to professional criticism rather than to pressure groups wielding clubs. Pressure groups have scored victories in getting one book banned and another altered. But isolated victories mean nothing without the support of professional opinion. . . . The substantial improvement in the treatment of racial and immigrant minorities in today's textbooks, compared with those published in the 1920's, has been far less the result of crusades against specific titles than of scholars' insistence upon the truth as they saw it.

It is true that there may be times when recognized scholars, limited by a specialist's viewpoint or swayed by prevailing winds of doctrine, will profess opinions even on their own subject that are open to criticism by an alert and perceptive citizenry. It is true that there may be times when it will be up to individuals or agencies concerned with the public good—or even with the interests of special groups—to air a situation which the profession itself is too slow to improve. It is true that there can be no monopoly where ideas are concerned and that a critic writing in a general magazine may sometimes give us a more broadly informed and socially responsible evaluation of a book than a scholar writing in a professional journal.

But, even so, the aim should be to discover and spread truth, not to deploy the greatest concentration of power and issue a ban. . . .

Criticism and discussion not only promise more real improvement than pressure tactics; they rule out of court the undemocratic and un-American textbook ban, so akin to the book-burning procedures of Nazis and Communists. In the meantime, however, it is clear we shall have to deal directly with the offensive of the book-burners.

The authors and publishers, whom one might expect to be the first line of defense, seem to have decided that discretion is the better part of valor. The authors of books under attack have said very little in reply to their critics, and their silence is apparently dictated by the publishers. . . . [The publisher of Frank A. Magruder's *American Government*] for example, has not fought back and has made significant changes in the dead author's text. . . .

Teachers have been more willing than authors and publishers to defend textbooks under attack. . . .

Teachers by themselves, and through their professional organizations, can go only so far. . . . A recent report on "The Freedom of the Public School Teacher" by the National Education Association reveals that teachers are becoming more and more subject to intimidation by various pressure groups. To an increasing extent, the NEA is looking to community action to support teachers against these attacks. This is a reasonable policy to pursue—the teachers, after all, have no place to turn but to the community—and one that should be endorsed by citizens interested in the welfare of their schools.

But it is not without its own perils: by inviting the community to participate in the defense of textbooks, is there not some risk of further inflaming tempers and ideologies, of further widening the gap between objective criticism and partisan denunciation? Is there not real danger of further involving teachers and teaching materials with sections of the community that may be ignorant, irresponsible, and all too willing themselves to flex the muscle of censorship? Might it not end with an ugly spectacle of stereotype pitted against stereotype, smear against smear? . . .

It is the scholar's role to rise above special interests. He is not always successful, but Professor [Preston H.] Epps [of the University of Wisconsin] . . . is quite right in the contention that "so far in our history, no group has been able to view our society and setup as objectively and intelligently as a group of devoted professional scholars. So far, we have wisely looked to such scholars to write the textbooks through which we want our youth to be introduced to the various fields of knowledge."

It will be necessary to remain constantly alert to see that a conflict over textbooks does not degenerate into a conflict of ideologies in which everyone will be on his own and will feel called upon to get in a sock. That way lies calamity. Qualified criticism, not pressure tactics, is the appropriate means of making one's views felt insofar as the writing and revision of text-books are concerned.

TEACHERS' MANIFESTO [9]

The National Council of Teachers of English is professionally obligated to stand publicly against dangers now threatening the important work for which its members are responsible in the classrooms of the nation. Prominent among these dangers are: (1) demands for the exclusion of certain books, periodicals, and other instructional materials from classrooms and libraries; (2) attacks upon the use of any material for any purpose from the writings of specific authors; (3) restrictions placed upon the kind of speakers who may address groups in schools and colleges; (4) denials of the right of classroom consideration by teachers and students of currently controversial topics. These limit freedom to know and to communicate, to learn and to teach. Together they could comprise an ominous prelude to thought control. . . .

Teachers of language and literature believe that school and college discussion of vital problems can help young people to discover the underlying causes of the problems, to examine possible solutions, and to suspend judgment; that it will deter them from taking up extreme and untenable views; and that it will discourage the more common—and more dangerous—drift toward apathy. Failure to face genuine issues in school and college brings loss of interest in education and a loss of respect for it. Young people ordinarily respond in a healthy way to frank discussion. If they hear all sides fairly presented, teachers, parents, and the general public can have confidence that students have taken a long stride toward the eventual exercise of good judgment. The goal education offers them is a steadily developing understanding of the life of their time, a reasonable and maturing response to this life, and full participation in it. . . .

[9] From *Censorship and Controversy*, pamphlet. National Council of Teachers of English. 8110 South Halsted Street. Chicago 30. 1953. p5-20. Reprinted by permission.

To attain or even to approach our goals as a people, teachers and students need access to all materials in books, periodicals, graphic representatives, recordings, motion pictures, and programs over the air that can contribute directly or indirectly to the particular projects of carefully planned courses at all levels of instruction. Nothing short of this will suffice. . . .

The National Council of Teachers of English believes firmly that Communist party doctrine, as avowed anywhere in the world today, is a fraudulent mask for an imperialism that seeks ultimately to overthrow our government by force and violence. It must be resisted resolutely at all points by each one of us. . . .

The second problem is the danger that ill-advised opponents of communism or other insidious enemies of our schools and colleges will seek to exploit the dangers of communism as an excuse for opposing any ideas which they do not like. Such persons may label as communistic any changes whatsoever in methods of teaching or use of instructional materials. They will use attacks upon communism as a means of making an easy living or of gaining notoriety and power. The techniques and procedures they employ undermine the basic freedoms we cherish and if permitted to flourish would ultimately destroy our way of life. . . .

It is the strong conviction of the National Council of Teachers of English that the schools and colleges of the nation must be on guard against communism and also against those persons who use the fear of communism as a pretext for vicious attacks upon the American educational system. . . .

In any particular instance of difference over the use of instructional materials, controversial topics, or speakers in schools and colleges, no single individual or group can make decisions alone. At least five parties may be actively concerned: teachers; students; school authorities, including boards of control; parents, other relatives, and friends of the students; and leaders of the community as represented by influential individuals and organizations. Only by a realization of the rights and duties of these groups and by their active and intelligent cooperation can healthy conditions in education be maintained. . . .

The teacher's responsibility is to present and to stress the total situation rather than a part of it, to see it in perspective. It is his professional duty to develop methods of weighing and comparing evidence and of moving toward tenable conclusions rather than of inculcating an easy orthodoxy or of leaving the student to reach decisions with no help. . . .

Students need an awareness of their classmates as individuals as well as members of groups. Under good guidance they have developed an open attitude towards their fellows in sports and other activities in which a premium is placed upon performance for the good of the group. Such an atmosphere in class, set by the teacher and the majority of the students, is a necessary condition for the discussion of many subjects and the consideration of many books. Such an atmosphere makes possible the use of materials that in less happy circumstances would cause difficulty. . . .

Administrators . . . should consider the merits of the criticism, its sources and possible motives; they should make decisions only after full inquiry and understanding of all sides. Frequently their function is to interpret the work of the school to people outside. Often they can satisfy a complainant by a candid explanation of the actual circumstances and the purpose of the work.

Administrators should not surrender to attacks or appease those acting on un-American premises. They should realize that many of those who attack schools most violently would not under any circumstance actively support education. A decision based on full evidence and made in a setting of reasonable discussion and democratic procedure is the goal. . . .

Parents play an important part in creating the conditions within which education is carried on, and their intelligent concern and active cooperation are especially important today in encouraging teachers to be courageous, forthright, and wise in handling controversial matters. Do parents really want their children taught by the conforming, the fearful, the unimaginative, the dull? . . .

The condition of a school as a rule reflects the atmosphere of its community and state; the condition of a college reflects the public from which it draws its support. There is consequently a general responsibility upon the leaders of a community, on the churches, newspapers, business firms, on all social and cultural organizations, and upon all professional people and others with a concern for public affairs to take an active stand for effective conduct of education at all levels.

THE CENSORS AND THE LIBRARIAN

EDITOR'S INTRODUCTION

The librarian's role in maintaining the free flow of ideas calls for full discussion of the pressures brought on him and how he meets them. The credo of the American librarian is set forth in the *Library Bill of Rights* and the American Library Association statement on labeling, opening this section, and is spelled out in more detail in the following statement by the Westchester Conference of librarians and publishers. A letter from the President of the United States reminds librarians of their duty to live up to these principles, and an official of the American Book Publishers Council contributes a reminder of the part played by books in the development of knowledge, character and citizenship.

A charge of pro-Communist "slanting" in a widely used guide to book selection is answered by a librarian. Two following articles describe an attempt to censor a librarian's selection of non-book material and how it was met.

A policy of limiting the circulation of books believed to contain subversive propaganda is put forward by the chief of a large public library and is criticized by two other prominent librarians. A description of a closely similar policy of segregating questionable material is followed by a defense of the library as a citadel of free communication, by a librarian who holds that all books in a collection should be equally accessible to the public. The book closes with a library school dean's reflections on the character of the book selection process.

LIBRARY BILL OF RIGHTS [1]

The Council of the American Library Association reaffirms its belief in the following basic policies which should govern the services of all libraries:

[1] Statement adopted by the Council of the American Library Association at its annual convention, 1939; reaffirmed, 1948. *American Library Association Bulletin*. 42:285. July-August 1948. Reprinted by permission.

1. As a responsibility of library service, books and other reading matter selected should be chosen for values of interest, information and enlightenment of all the people for the community. In no case should any book be excluded because of the race or nationality, or the political or religious views of the writer.

2. There should be the fullest practicable provision of material presenting all points of view concerning the problems and issues of our times, international, national, and local; and books or other reading matter of sound factual authority should not be proscribed or removed from library shelves because of partisan or doctrinal disapproval.

3. Censorship of books, urged or practiced by volunteer arbiters of morals or political opinion or by organizations that would establish a coercive concept of Americanism, must be challenged by libraries in maintenance of their responsibility to provide public information and enlightenment through the printed word.

4. Libraries should enlist the cooperation of allied groups in the fields of science, of education, and of book publishing in resisting all abridgment of the free access to ideas and full freedom of expression that are the tradition and heritage of Americans.

5. As an institution of education for democratic living, the library should welcome the use of its meeting rooms for socially useful and cultural activities and discussions of current public questions. Such meeting places should be available on equal terms to all groups in the community regardless of the beliefs and affiliations of their members.

[By official action of the Council on February 3, 1951, the Library Bill of Rights was interpreted to apply to all materials and media of communication used or collected by libraries.[2] —Ed.]

[2] *American Library Association Bulletin.* 47:485. November 1953.

ALA STATEMENT ON LABELING [3]

In view of our own convictions and those of other practicing librarians whose counsel we sought, the Committee on Intellectual Freedom recommends to the ALA Council the following policy with respect to labeling library materials:

Librarians should not use the technique of labeling as a means of predisposing readers against library materials for the following reasons:

1. Although totalitarian states find it easy and even proper, according to their ethics, to establish criteria for judging publications as "subversive," injustice and ignorance rather than justice and enlightenment result from such practices, and the American Library Association has a responsibility to take a stand against the establishment of such criteria in a democratic state.

2. Libraries do not advocate the ideas found in their collections. The presence of a magazine or book in a library does not indicate an endorsement of its contents by the library.

3. No one person should take the responsibility of labeling publications. No sizable group of persons would be likely to agree either on the types of material which should be labeled or the sources of information which should be regarded with suspicion. As a practical consideration, a librarian who labeled a book or magazine pro-Communist might be sued for libel.

4. Labeling is an attempt to prejudice the reader, and as such, it is a censor's tool.

5. Labeling violates the spirit of the Library Bill of Rights.

6. Although we are all agreed that communism is a threat to the free world, if materials are labeled to pacify one group, there is no excuse for refusing to label any item in the Library's collection. Because communism, fascism, or other authoritarianisms tend to suppress ideas and attempt to coerce individuals to conform to a specific ideology, American librarians must be opposed to such "isms." We are, then, anti-Communist, but we are also opposed to any other group which aims at closing any path to knowledge.

[3] Recommendations unanimously adopted by the American Library Association Council, July 13, 1951. *American Library Association Bulletin.* 45:242. July-August 1951. Reprinted by permission.

THE FREEDOM TO READ [4]

The freedom to read is essential to our democracy. It is under attack. Private groups and public authorities in various parts of the country are working to remove books from sale, to censor textbooks, to label "controversial" books, to distribute lists of "objectionable" books or authors, and to purge libraries.

These actions apparently rise from a view that our national tradition of free expression is no longer valid; that censorship and suppression are needed to avoid the subversion of politics and the corruption of morals. We, as citizens devoted to the use of books and as librarians and publishers responsible for disseminating them, wish to assert the public interest in the preservation of the freedom to read.

We are deeply concerned about these attempts at suppression. Most such attempts rest on a denial of the fundamental premise of democracy: that the ordinary citizen, by exercising his critical judgment, will accept the good and reject the bad. The censors, public and private, assume that they should determine what is good and what is bad for their fellow citizens.

We trust Americans to recognize propaganda, and to reject obscenity. We do not believe they need the help of censors to assist them in this task. We do not believe they are prepared to sacrifice their heritage of a free press in order to be "protected" against what others think may be bad for them. We believe they still favor free enterprise in ideas and expression.

We are aware, of course, that books are not alone in being subjected to efforts at suppression. We are aware that these efforts are related to a larger pattern of pressures being brought against education, the press, films, radio, and television. The problem is not only one of actual censorship. The shadow of fear cast by these pressures leads, we suspect, to an even larger voluntary curtailment of expression by those who seek to avoid controversy.

[4] A statement prepared by the Westchester Conference of the American Library Association and the American Book Publishers Council—May 2 and 3, 1953; endorsed by the American Book Publishers Council, Board of Directors; the American Library Association Council; the American Booksellers Association Board of Directors; the National Commission for the Defense of Democracy through Education, appointed by the National Education Association of the U.S.A.; the Book Manufacturers' Institute. *Wilson Library Bulletin.* 28:60-2. September 1953.

Such pressure toward conformity is perhaps natural to a time of uneasy change and pervading fear. Especially when so many of our apprehensions are directed against an ideology, the expression of a dissident idea becomes a thing feared in itself, and we tend to move against it as against a hostile deed, with suppression.

And yet suppression is never more dangerous than in such a time of social tension. Freedom has given the United States the elasticity to endure strain. Freedom keeps open the path of novel and creative solutions, and enables change to come by choice. Every silencing of a heresy, every enforcement of an orthodoxy, diminishes the toughness and resilience of our society and leaves it the less able to deal with stress.

Now as always in our history, books are among our greatest instruments of freedom. They are almost the only means for making generally available ideas or manners of expression that can initially command only a small audience. They are the natural medium for the new idea and the untried voice, from which come the original contributions to social growth. They are essential to the extended discussion which serious thought requires, and to the accumulation of knowledge and ideas into organized collections.

We believe that free communication is essential to the preservation of a free society and a creative culture. We believe that these pressures toward conformity present the danger of limiting the range and variety of inquiry and expression on which our democracy and our culture depend. We believe that every American community must jealously guard the freedom to publish and to circulate, in order to preserve its own freedom to read. We believe that publishers and librarians have a profound responsibility to give validity to that freedom to read by making it possible for the reader to choose freely from a variety of offerings.

The freedom to read is guaranteed by the Constitution. Those with faith in free men will stand firm on these constitutional guarantees of essential rights and will exercise the responsibilities that accompany these rights.

We therefore affirm these propositions:

1. It is in the public interest for publishers and librarians to make available the widest diversity of views and expressions, including those which are unorthodox or unpopular with the majority.

Creative thought is by definition new, and what is new is different. ' The bearer of every new thought is a rebel until his idea is refined and tested. Totalitarian systems attempt to maintain themselves in power by the ruthless suppression of any concept which challenges the established orthodoxy. The power of a democratic system to adapt to change is vastly strengthened by the freedom of its citizens to choose widely from among conflicting opinions offered freely to them. To stifle every nonconformist idea at birth would mark the end of the democratic process. Furthermore, only through the constant activity of weighing and selecting can the democratic mind attain the strength demanded by times like these. We need to know not only what we believe but why we believe it.

2. Publishers and librarians do not need to endorse every idea or presentation contained in the books they make available. It would conflict with the public interest for them to establish their own political, moral, or esthetic views as the sole standard for determining what books should be published or circulated.

Publishers and librarians serve the educational process by helping to make available knowledge and ideas required for the growth of the mind and the increase of learning. They do not foster education by imposing as mentors the patterns of their own thought. The people should have the freedom to read and consider a broader range of ideas than those that may be held by any single librarian or publisher or government or church. It is

wrong that what one man can read should be confined to what
another thinks proper.

3. It is contrary to the public interest for publishers
or librarians to determine the acceptability of a book
solely on the basis of the personal history or political
affiliations of the author.

A book should be judged as a book. No art or literature
can flourish if it is to be measured by the political views or
private lives of its creators. No society of free men can flourish
which draws up lists of writers to whom it will not listen, whatever they may have to say.

4. The present laws dealing with obscenity should
be vigorously enforced. Beyond that, there is no place
in our society for extralegal efforts to coerce the taste of
others, to confine adults to the reading matter deemed
suitable for adolescents, or to inhibit the efforts of writers
to achieve artistic expression.

To some, much of modern literature is shocking. But is not
much of life itself shocking? We cut off literature at the source
if we prevent serious artists from dealing with the stuff of life.
Parents and teachers have a responsibility to prepare the young
to meet the diversity of experiences in life to which they will be
exposed, as they have a responsibility to help them learn to think
critically for themselves. These are affirmative responsibilities,
not discharged simply by preventing them from reading works
for which they are not yet prepared. In these matters taste dif-
ers, and taste cannot be legislated; nor can machinery be devised
which will suit the demands of one group without limiting the
freedom of others. We deplore the catering to the immature,
the retarded, or the maladjusted taste. But those concerned with
freedom have the responsibility of seeing to it that each individual book or publication, whatever its contents, price, or

method of distribution, is dealt with in accordance with due process of law.

5. It is not in the public interest to force a reader to accept with any book the prejudgment of a label characterizing the book or author as subversive or dangerous.

The idea of labeling supposes the existence of individuals or groups with wisdom to determine by authority what is good or bad for the citizen. It supposes that each individual must be directed in making up his mind about the ideas he examines. But Americans do not need others to do their thinking for them.

6. It is the responsibility of publishers and librarians, as guardians of the people's freedom to read, to contest encroachments upon that freedom by individuals or groups seeking to impose their own standards or tastes upon the community at large.

It is inevitable in the give and take of the democratic process that the political, the moral, or the esthetic concepts of an individual or group will occasionally collide with those of another individual or group. In a free society each individual is free to determine for himself what he wishes to read, and each group is free to determine what it will recommend to its freely associated members. But no group has the right to take the law into its own hands, and to impose its own concepts of politics or morality upon other members of a democratic society. Freedom is no freedom if it is accorded only to the accepted and the inoffensive.

7. It is the responsibility of publishers and librarians to give full meaning to the freedom to read by providing books that enrich the quality of thought and expression. By the exercise of this affirmative responsibility, bookmen can demonstrate that the answer to a bad book is a good one, the answer to a bad idea is a good one.

The freedom to read is of little consequence when expended on the trivial; it is frustrated when the reader cannot obtain matter fit for his purpose. What is needed is not only the absence of restraint, but the positive provision of opportunity for the people to read the best that has been thought and said. Books are the major channel by which the intellectual inheritance is handed down, and the principal means of its testing and growth. The defense of their freedom and integrity, and the enlargement of their service to society, requires of all bookmen the utmost of their faculties, and deserves of all citizens the fullest of their support.

We state these propositions neither lightly nor as easy generalizations. We here stake out a lofty claim for the value of books. We do so because we believe that they are good, possessed of enormous variety and usefulness, worthy of cherishing and keeping free. We realize that the application of these propositions may mean the dissemination of ideas and manners of expression that are repugnant to many persons. We do not state these propositions in the comfortable belief that what people read is unimportant. We believe rather that what people read is deeply important; that ideas can be dangerous; but that the suppression of ideas is fatal to a democratic society. Freedom itself is a dangerous way of life, but it is ours.

LIBRARIANS SERVE LIBERTY [5]

Our librarians serve the precious liberties of our nation: freedom of inquiry, freedom of the spoken and the written word, freedom of exchange of ideas.

Upon these clear principles, democracy depends for its very life, for they are the great sources of knowledge and enlightenment. And knowledge—full, unfettered knoweldge of its own heritage, of freedom's enemies, of the whole world of men and ideas—this knowledge is a free people's surest strength.

[5] From a letter by President Dwight D. Eisenhower, read at the American Library Association Council meeting, Los Angeles, June 26, 1953. *Wilson Library Bulletin*. 28:59-60. September 1953.

The converse is just as surely true. A democracy smugly disdainful of new ideas would be a sick democracy. A democracy chronically fearful of new ideas would be a dying democracy.

For all these reasons, we must in these times be intelligently alert not only to the fanatic cunning of Communist conspiracy—but also to the grave dangers in meeting fanaticism with ignorance. For, in order to fight totalitarians who exploit the ways of freedom to serve their own ends, there are some zealots who—with more wrath than wisdom—would adopt a strangely unintelligent course. They would try to defend freedom by denying freedom's friends the opportunity of studying communism in its entirety—its plausibilities, its falsities, its weaknesses.

But we know that freedom cannot be served by the devices of the tyrant. As it is an ancient truth that freedom cannot be legislated into existence, so it is no less obvious that freedom cannot be censored into existence. And any who act as if freedom's defenses are to be found in suppression and suspicion and fear confess a doctrine that is alien to America.

The libraries of America are and must ever remain the homes of free, inquiring minds. To them, our citizens—of all ages and races, of all creeds and political persuasions—must ever be able to turn with clear confidence that there they can freely seek the whole truth, unwarped by fashion and uncompromised by expediency. For in such whole and healthy knowledge alone are to be found and understood those majestic truths of man's nature and destiny that prove, to each succeeding generation, the validity of freedom.

FREEDOM AND BOOKS [5]

Our kind of government requires that all men be free to speak and to hear—to write and to read—as they choose. It requires this because it is dedicated to the proposition that all men are created equal and share equally in the responsibility for public decisions: in other words to the proposition that each man

---

[5] From an address by Dan Lacy, managing director, American Book Publishers Council, to the Georgia State Library Association, St. Simons Island, October 24, 1953. 12p. Mimeographed. The Council. 2 West 46th Street. New York 26. 1953. Reprinted by permission.

makes up his own mind after a free debate among alternatives. If there is a limitation on the freedom of discussion, then the decision is no longer wholly in the hands of the people, but to that degree in the hands of those who have power to limit the debate. . . .

Even if it were not necessary to every decision of our government, indeed even if it were politically utterly futile, still the freedom to speak and be heard, the freedom to inquire and learn is part of the meaning of life itself. A man fearful to speak as he thinks, to ask his own questions, seek his own answers and make up his own mind, is not a whole man. . . .

However, the service of freedom through books presents problems far more complex than those of overt censorship itself. . . . Two major developments have brought books and freedom into a much more complex and important relationship.

One of these developments is the increasing reliance of the citizen on second-hand information. The second is the rise of the mass media of communication. A century, even a half-century ago, the decisions which government faced were concerned with matters of everyday experience, and the voter could understand and participate in the issues before him on the basis of his personal knowledge. But today how he votes and the views he voices to his congressman necessarily involve remote and unfamiliar matters: the dollar balance of Great Britain, the adequacy of potential defenses against atomic bombing, the stability of the Japanese economy, the workability of the excess profits tax. The citizen acts from day to day—not only as a voter but in making his own personal and business decisions—on second-hand knowledge, on things he has read or heard and which he cannot test against his own experience. . . . If he hears only one side of the story about national or international issues it is now almost impossible for him to supply correctives from his first-hand knowledge.

At the same time there have arisen new phenomena of communication: the mass-circulated magazines and newspapers, press associations, radio, TV, films. Most people rely primarily on these for their image of the complex world in which they live. Each of them requires a major capital investment, each has to be assured of a mass audience, especially those supported by advertising, each fears to offend. Each is hence impelled toward a careful neutralism and no sharp clash with currently accepted ideas. Moreover none can afford to deal at length and carefully with problems in which only a few thousand or a few tens of thousands of people may be keenly interested. And none lends itself to a user's own choice and inquiry. . . .

Generally honestly and fairly administered, these mass media do an indispensable job of pumping out current news and ideas, without which our complicated society could not function. But they do not serve the need of the man who wants to dig into something for himself, find out the other side, explore the problem on his own. And more urgently than ever, our society to remain free needs such an opportunity for the inquiring citizen to go find out for himself. It is our one great protection against the one idea, against the pressures of conscious or unconscious propaganda, against the closed mind of conformity.

This means books. It means books, where you have time to develop a thought at length and not in a capsule. It means books, which can deal with complicated sets of facts. It means books, which with no sponsors or advertisers to worry about and no mass market to keep happy can take sides, can present unpopular views, can "think otherwise," can oppose the stubborn and disagreeable fact to the popular fallacy, can keep going that debate which we need always to keep our minds tough and free.

And it means a lot of books. It means books about all problems, and books on both sides. It means a collection of books where a man can come to find out for himself about a problem he meets and his country meets, and where too he can find among a varied company of great minds the communion he needs to achieve the enfranchisement of his own spirit. It means, in short, a library. It means you.

And so today, if books are to serve freedom as they must, it is not enough that they be protected from censorship. The use of books is in their reading, and no man is truly free to read if he has no access to an adequate body of books. Freedom to read must be not so much protected as achieved. You, as librarians, work at the heart of the problem. An adequate public library system, extending throughout the country and giving library service to the tens of millions now without it, is as essential to the preservation of freedom today as was a free public school system in Thomas Jefferson's day.

The maintenance and extension of a library system adequate to the contemporary needs of freedom can, of course, be done only with public funds, and here public policy has to deal with a harder problem than that of censorship. In the latter case you can deny the right of the government to suppress any voice, and call on the First Amendment for your protection. But in the case of libraries, the role of the government—federal, state or local—is positive, not negative. It must take affirmative action to make books available, and since it cannot make everything available it must achieve a selection.

This exposes the librarian to pressures beyond the protection of the First Amendment—to unofficial citizens' committees and church patriotic organizations who demand that the library in the selection of its holdings reflect their ideas of what is right. . . .

The most frequent form of current attack is based on the presence in libraries of books by or about authors who are accused of membership in subversive organizations. . . . The lists of authors used usually include a number of actual Communists and a very much larger number of authors whose offense is that at some time or another they belonged to an organization that at some time or other was held by someone to be subversive. This criterion could be used to exclude a very high proportion of authors, for the creative artist in any field is by nature a rebel. He protests against things and he is likely to join organizations that protest against things, and these are the kinds of organizations that Communists like to infiltrate. He is also likely to be the first man to get out of such an organization as soon as he sees that it is trying to tell him how to think, for the creative mind is a stubborn and intractable one, not readily amenable to any discipline and least of all to that of communism. To remove from a public library all the books capable of being listed on this basis would be to gut it of a precious and indispensable part of its holdings. . . .

Very frequently attacks from this source will not demand the removal of books that are in libraries, but rather the inclusion of a balancing number of books representing the point of view of the complaining group. . . . Though a very high proportion of the books recommended by such groups are likely to be vicious and scurrilous works of poor quality, and though obviously no library can function if the responsibilty for book selection is taken out of the hands of the staff and trustees who are responsible for services to the community, and made subject to the pressures of many kinds of groups of the right or of the left who want to use it as a channel for their own views, I would still urge thoughtful consideration of requests that argue for the inclusion of books in the library rather than their exclusion. The mere fact that you or I disagree with a book is no more reason for keeping it out of the library than that anybody else does. . . .

What should a librarian do when confronted by a sincere, if misguided group of citizens who want to disturb the selection policies of the library by the pressure of a special interest? In the first place, the good librarian has acted before this happens. The good librarian has been working with her board of trustees and with other good citizens in the community all along to help them realize that it is the whole purpose of a library to extend the range of ideas that are discussed and debated and that if it does not include controversial books on both sides of questions, then it is failing its function. . . .

In the second place, realize that the point of view represented in this sort of attack on public libraries commands no respectable support when the issues are fully debated and aired. As Vice President Nixon, speaking at the American Legion Convention in St. Louis last month, pointed out: "We must all recognize that the right to advocate unpopular ideas is part of our American tradition." . . .

It is a part of the convictions we all live by that free books and free men go together. Your institutions are the means of bringing them and keeping them together, and no service to freedom is more important at the root than yours.

LIBRARIANS' "SLANTED" GUIDE [6]

Helen E. Haines is the dean of American librarians. For half a century or more she helped direct the growth of the American Library Association. Her love of books, her wide reading, her enthusiasm, her mastery of the library arts, her skill as a teacher, lecturer and writer—all these combined to make her a key figure among those who operate and direct our thousands of libraries. Her views and recommendations on book selections have carried—and still carry—tremendous weight. She is, so to speak, the librarians' librarian.

A few months ago Columbia University Press brought out a new and revised edition of Miss Haines's *magnum opus, Living With Books.* The new edition, wrote Miss Haines, was needed "to show the ever-enlarging flow of books through our own times as manifestation of, and accompaniment to, the surging streams of history we are living in." . . .

To all who have known Miss Haines's long and honorable career, her objectivity as well as her open-mindedness were beyond question. Her recommendations on newer books—as on older ones—therefore carried tremendous authority. Since it was first published in 1935, *Living With Books* has become the bible of librarians everywhere. In the ten thousand or more public, private, high school and college libraries of the United States, no textbook for librarians is more highly regarded. . . .

I have read carefully both the original 1935 edition and the 1950 revised edition [of Miss Haines's book]. I can appreciate the enthusiasm of librarians for this textbook. It is well organized and filled with information of value to every library specialist. It evaluates hundreds of volumes. Each chapter has a list of recommended books. Above all, the book is easy to read. No wonder librarians swear by it.

There is, however, a profound—and dangerous—difference between the 1935 edition and that of 1950. For at some point in the intervening years Miss Haines "discovered" Soviet Russia

[6] From "A Slanted Guide to Library Selections," by Oliver Carlson, public relations counsel and author of *Handbook of Propaganda. Freeman.* 2:239-42. January 14, 1952. Reprinted by permission.

and the Communist philosophy. Like all new converts, she has lost no opportunity in revising her book to play up her discovery. In fact, the major impression I get from a comparison of the original with the revised edition is the strong pro-Soviet bias of the latter. Miss Haines may think she is still objective, but in fact she has now become a propagandist for the Stalinist way of life. . . .

In the 1935 edition of *Living With Books,* "communism" was not listed in the index (despite the fact that communism had been a major issue in world politics for nearly eighteen years). In the 1950 edition there are 31 items under that heading. The USSR, as such, was unlisted in 1935. There were 17 items under it in 1950. Marxian philosophy was unlisted in the first edition. There are 36 items under that head in the new edition. . . .

Librarians are warned by Miss Haines of the current "hysteria" against all books and publications friendly to communism. Political censorship, she insists, "has drawn strength from postwar reaction." She is determined to stop the "witch hunts" and "book burnings." The picture she paints is so far from the truth that it might well have been taken from any one of the leading pro-Communist journals or from the writings of any one of the fellow-traveling authors she recommends and endorses.

An "essentially nationalistic" reaction, we are told,

rose in the late 1940's to a nation-wide hysteria. "Treason" was read into acts, associations and thoughts arbitrarily defined as "disloyal"; books were suppressed or removed from libraries. Scholars accused of "liberal thoughts" were dismissed from colleges and universities; "loyalty tests" and "loyalty boards" were set in operation for workers of every grade in the framework of federal, state, county and municipal service. In spite of protest and resistant action by writers, publishers, teachers, scientists, librarians, many leaders in social and political thought, and a minority of newspapers, sanity and fair dealing seemed in eclipse. . . .

Let us consider more specifically those books and authors selected for praise by Miss Haines. In the field of drama, for example, only one book on motion picture and play writing is given unstinted praise. This is *The Theory and Techniques of Play Writing and Screen Writing,* by John Howard Lawson, which she terms an "exhaustive, illuminating and explorative study." The damage done to the motion picture industry by Lawson and his fellow Communists in the Screen Writers Guild for nearly fifteen years has been documented by the testimony of Morrie Ryskind, Fred Niblo, Richard McCaulley, Howard Emmett Rogers, James K. McGuinness and many other leading screen writers. Lawson, be it remembered, was both the hatchet man and the commissar for the Hollywood Muscovites. But Miss Haines makes no mention of these facts. Instead she recommends his 1949 revised edition because:

> It adds a comprehensive section covering in brilliant, incisive analysis the development and problems of the motion picture from its American beginnings in 1908; and the whole text, by introduction and summations, has been given a fresh impact of immediacy in its penetrating exposition of the opposed ideological, social and economic influences that find expression in present-day dramatic art.

Miss Haines's chapter on Poetry closes with a stirring appeal to librarians to know and make available to the public "the Marxist classic, *Illusion and Reality,* by Christopher Caudwell." This, we are told, is "a seminal volume . . . which . . . sets up milestones new to most American readers as it traces the course of poetry from the primitive past through an obscured present to an idealized future." She calls the book "a work of creative genius and encyclopedic range. . . ."

In her revised section on literature, Miss Haines labels anti-Communist George Orwell's powerful satire *1984* as "paranoia in literature." But she hails . . . Norman Mailer's *The Naked and the Dead* as high-grade fiction with its "grim, overpowering evocation of inhumanity, corruption and military fascism in the American capture of a small Japanese island in the Pacific." . . .

Her chapter on Religion and Philosophy has been revised to permit a rather detailed and flattering exposition of Marxian philosophy. Librarians are especially urged to use John Somerville's *Soviet Philosophy,* which is "sympathetic in approach, authoritative in background, and opening valuable extensive material for comprehensive study." Professor Sidney Hook and other competent philosophers insist that Somerville's book is deliberately slanted to paint a glowing but untrue picture of Soviet theory in practice. Miss Haines makes no mention of

Hook or any other philosopher who is critical of communism except Bertrand Russell (whom she could not very well ignore).

Librarians are urged to put more books on their shelves which represent the Communist point of view because "it must be remembered that any philosophy of life, to be understood, must be approached with a certain amount of sympathetic imagination." Furthermore, says the author, "unqualified attack, reprobation, and denunciation are usually strongly represented in general library selection in this subject." . . .

When discussing current books on international relations, sociology and political science Miss Haines stacks her cards more deliberately than anywhere else on behalf of the forces of Stalinism. It is all done in a very nice way. For example, take this statement:

> Strong antagonism—personal, ideological, or political—dominating descriptive and interpretative books on Soviet Russia (John Fischer, V. A. Kravchenko are examples) should be balanced by more sympathetic, equally authentic work, such as that of Albert Rhys Williams, Edgar Snow, Hewlett Johnson and Walter Duranty. . . .

Among the recommended "Fifty Books of the Times Indicating Trends and Tendencies" there is listed *only one* which is critical of the growing trend to Statism: Hayek's *The Road to Serfdom.*

To counterbalance this single book, we are given: Frederick Schuman's *Soviet Policy at Home and Abroad;* E. J. Simmons's *USSR Handbook;* Anna Louise Strong's *Tomorrow's China;* H. P. Beck's *Men Who Control Our Universities;* Harold J. Laski's *The American Democracy*; John Somerville's *The Philosophy of Peace;* Carey McWilliams's *Brothers Under the Skin* and *A Mask for Privilege;* Francis Williams's *Socialist Britain;* Henry Sigerist's *Medicine and Human Welfare;* Nathan Straus's *The Seven Myths of Housing;* Henry Wallace's *Sixty Million Jobs.* . . .

"Even in limited collections" of the smaller libraries, advises Miss Haines:

> there should also be authentic exposition of Marxian doctrine from the Marxist viewpoint, the tractates by Lenin and Stalin which are standard expressions of Soviet theory and practice, and Sidney and

Beatrice Webb's *Soviet Communism: A New Civilization?,* which since 1936 in its various editions, has been basic to study of the subject by American readers. Andrei Vishinsky's massive, militant exposition of *The Law of the Soviet State,* though too expensive for smaller general collections, is of foundational value to any reader who wishes to understand the structure of the Soviet state. . . .

One looks in vain through this massive book for the works of David Dallin, William Henry Chamberlin and a host of other experts on Russia or the Far East. Not a single volume on life behind the Iron Curtain in the satellite countries is mentioned except Robert St. John's pro-Tito *The Silent People Speak.*

Nowhere is mention made of any study on the slave labor camps of Soviet Russia, or the eye-witness reports of those who have fled from behind the Iron Curtain. Nor is a solitary book listed (of the many written) which tells of the rape of Poland and the Baltic States. Isaac Deutscher's faintly critical biography of Stalin is on the recommended list. Not so the monumental study by Boris Souvarine. Instead, Miss Haines warns her readers that there are too many

present-day biographies motivated by intense political or ideological partisanship and overshadowed by personal antagonisms (as in *The Red Prussian: The Life and Legend of Karl Marx,* by Leopold Schwarzschild, and in the deadly personal enmity that imparts unintended ironic flavor to the biography of Stalin by Trotsky). . . .

The half-century of good work on behalf of library science performed by Helen E. Haines will long remain to her credit. But her late espousal of communism, and her attempt to boost its literature, are to be sincerely regretted. To attempt to stack our public library shelves with the works of men and women who are dedicated to destroying our freedom—without clearly and unequivocally indicating this fact—is to undermine the very purposes of the American Library Association.

Miss Haines has never given her name to any of the Communist front organizations. She has probably never even gone to any of their meetings. . . . She is the perfect "innocent." Like so many muddled European and American intellectuals, she has mistaken the fine and noble phrases of Communist propaganda for Communist reality. It is time that she—and they—stopped living with books long enough to see the world as it really is.

REPLY TO CARLSON [7]

The January 14, 1952, issue of *The Freeman* contains an article by Oliver Carlson, "A Slanted Guide to Library Selections," attacking the 1950 edition of *Living With Books* by Helen Haines. . . .

Carlson first stresses the enormous influence which he feels Helen Haines has on library book selection. He then states he has "read carefully both the original 1935 edition and the 1950 revised edition." This convinced him that "at some point in the intervening years Miss Haines 'discovered' Soviet Russia and the Communist philosophy." In proof of this he cites the fact that the index to the old edition does not mention communism but that the 1950 edition has 31 items under that heading, that the USSR was not listed in the old index but has 17 items in the new, and that Marxian philosophy has 36 items listed in the new index but none in the old.

The connection between the number of times a subject is mentioned in an index and the author's views on that subject is not quite clear to me, but a comparison of the two indexes will show that the new one which contains 40 pages is more extensive than the old edition, which has only 30, the latter being essentially an author and title guide with a few general subject entries.

Leaving the index, Carlson next quotes five lines from the end of a long paragraph on book reviewing. I give the entire paragraph from pages 108-109 of *Living With Books* with the lines Carlson quoted in italics.

There are no rigid rules binding critical judgment to a given formula. In book reviewing, as in every human activity, there are "many men of many minds." For literary criticism is essentially an attempt to define the qualities of a certain piece of writing and to decide whether or not it has been well done. The decision will be influenced by the standards of judgment that the individual critic accepts and applies— whether traditional and erudite, as in the critical writings of Paul Elmer More, or vigorously factual and ironic, as in the reviewing of Bernard

[7] From an article by Elinor S. Earle, head of Reference Division, Akron (Ohio) Public Library. *American Library Association Bulletin.* 46:105-10. April 1952. Reprinted by permission.

De Voto, or intellectualized and psychoanalytical, as in much of the work of Edmund Wilson. Beyond certain boundary lines, however, critical judgment does not function, and we enter a region of bad taste and fatuous opinion, where adult infantilism seeks and finds books of its own caliber. Within the canons that establish literature as an art, though all critics agree on fundamentals, not many think alike. In all his years of writing [William Dean] Howells was a champion of realism and disliked romantic literature. Stevenson loved romance and continually pleads for it in his charming critical essays. Paul Elmer More was indifferent to the most vital and significant modern literature. Stuart Sherman in his earlier critical work sharply attacked writers whose powers he later recognized. The intense anti-Puritanism of Ludwig Lewisohn leaves its tinge on his critical judgments. Individual convictions of political or social faith, personal intensities of partisanship, find violent expression in contemporary reviewing. *In the literature of the war and postwar years the clash of nationalisms, the conflict of ideologies kindled impassioned warfare; and the great reviewing combat arena of the period is that devoted to books about Russia. Balanced judgment and fair understanding were obscured and the scales of American public opinion were weighted by prejudice and hostility of a strong anti-Soviet "bloc" of reviewers, so that impartial, adequate book selection in this field deteriorated in many library collections.*

By quoting only the concluding lines and by preceding them with his own statement that "the tremendous power wielded by book reviewers who were apologists and defenders of the Soviet government and communism has been reported in detail by several writers during the past year," Carlson gives the impression that Haines is an ardent Soviet partisan.

A similar false impression is conveyed by Carlson's quoting of Miss Haines on censorship. In a long chapter on the book trade, the history of printing and copyright, Haines gives two pages on the history of censorship, including examples of book burning in China in 213 B.C. . . . The actual passage on political censorship in the 1950 edition runs as follows (the part italicized is that quoted by Carlson):

Political censorship, at times quiescent but never extinct, has drawn renewed strength (as was true after the First World War) from postwar reaction. Essentially nationalistic, focusing on so-called "communistic doctrine," "Anti-Americanism," and "subversive literature," strengthened by deepening hostility to Soviet Russia, and intensified by development of the U.S.-Soviet "cold war," it rose *in the late 1940's to a nation-wide hysteria. "Treason" was read into acts, associations, and thoughts arbitrarily defined as "disloyal"; books were suppressed or removed from libraries. Scholars accused of "liberal thoughts" were dismissed from colleges and universities; "loyalty tests" and "loyalty boards" were set in operation for workers of every grade in the framework of federal, state, county and municipal service. In spite of protest and resistant action by writers, publishers, teachers, scientists, librarians, many leaders in social and political thought, and a minority of newspapers, sanity and fair dealing seemed in eclipse.*

In both political and moralistic aspects, censorship can become a dangerous and destructive influence, not only in publishing and book-selling, but in library service, in education, and in intellectual and cultural life. In library book selection, problems are constantly encountered that arise directly from traditional acceptances of its principles and methods.

Carlson states that "when discussing current books on international relations, sociology and political science, Miss Haines stacks her cards more deliberately than anywhere else on behalf of the forces of Stalinism." The first quotation he gives as an example comes not from the section referred to, but from the chapter on Travel. I give the paragraph as it is, with the lines Carlson quoted italicized:

Point of view: The trustworthy traveler is fair-minded, tolerant, and interested. A biased point of view or strong personal prejudices are among the most common defects of travel literature. Only when a book has great vividness or unusual value from other aspects are these defects offset. There should always be sympathy, or at least fair play, toward the life the traveler depicts. An aggressive Protestant is unlikely to interpret a Roman Catholic country with entire fairness. A militant WCTU [Women's Christian Temperance Union] tourist should not describe a French vintage festival. A highly antiseptic sanitarian will probably be blind to the picturesque aspects of life among the gypsies. Katherine Mayo's *Mother India* is a devastating example of reformist ardor condemning an entire ancient civilization for a recognized and age-old evil. *Strong antagonisms—personal, ideological, or political—dominating descriptive and interpretative books on Soviet Russia (John Fischer, V. A. Kravchenko are examples) should be balanced by more sympathetic, equally authentic work, such as that of Albert Rhys Williams, Edgar Snow, Hewlett Johnson, and Walter Duranty."* . . .

Carlson's quotation from Haines in regard to the need for authentic exposition of Marxian doctrine from the Marxist point of view would be much clearer if given in context. I give the passage with Carlson's quotation italicized (p. 371):

The irreconcilable antagonisms that rage today through the once arid regions of sociology are akin to those that for centuries inspired the wars of religion. To understand an issue, whatever it may be, "the other side" must be known and weighed by reason and an adequate sense of values, not by passion. Thus, in the locked battle between capitalism and communism that now divides the two great world powers, materials of both defense and attack must be freely available for public information and study. This responsibility should be maintained in library selection. Even in limited collections, besides literature that upholds American principles of democracy and freedom, *there should be authentic exposition of Marxian doctrine from the Marxist viewpoint, the tractates by Lenin and Stalin which are standard expressions of "Soviet theory and practice, and Sidney and Beatrice Webb's* Soviet Communism: a New Civilization, *which since 1936, in its various editions, has been basic to study of the subject by American readers. Andrei Vishinsky's massive, militant exposition of* The Law of the Soviet State, *though too expensive for smaller general collections, is of fundamental value to any reader who wishes to understand the structure of the Soviet state and the* uncompromising dogmatism of Soviet political and economic doctrine. This is probably the most notable volume in the "Russian Translations Project," organized in 1944 by the American Council of Learned Societies (with the aid of a Rockefeller Foundation subsidy and publication by Macmillan) and devoted to the translation into English of significant Russian works in the fields of the humanities and the social sciences which provide an insight into Russian life and thought.

By lopping off the concluding phrases of the sentence quoted, it is obvious that Carlson conveys a meaning not intended by Haines. . . .

Carlson often adds emotional interpretations to factual statements by Haines. For example, he claims that Miss Haines "is angry even with those old 'liberal' standbys, the *Nation* and the *New Republic*," and that "she laments, too, the passing of the *New Masses.*" Actually, Miss Haines names the two former publications as representing "radical and liberal thought, in politics, art and drama, as well as in literature" and then adds that "both jettisoned much of their cargo of former consistent opinion under the fierce storm of anti-Communist feeling engendered by the 'cold war.' " (Haines, p. 114.) In the same paragraph she mentions the *New Masses* as the former representative of "the extreme left wing" and then adds that it was merged with *Mainstream* to form *Masses and Mainstream*. Carlson accuses Miss Haines of failing to make it clear that this publication is "Stalinist," but it is clearly identified as Marxian. . . .

It must be remembered that *Living With Books* contains 610 pages. Mr. Carlson's strenuous efforts to prove his point result in his discovery of a very small number of titles listed which may or may not have a Communist bias. If Miss Haines had not included some titles of this nature she, herself, would have been guilty of suppressing information about an important and influential doctrine which, although it is distasteful to Americans, exists in our world.

THE PEORIA CASE [8]

Peoria . . . is a very active center of American Legion activities. . . . Peoria Post Number 2 maintains an extremely active "Americanism" committee, which occupies its time ferreting out "subversive" tendencies in much the same fashion as its counterpart in the House of Representatives. It concerns itself, of course, with the textbooks used in the local schools; but it has gone beyond this common Legion activity to attack the public library's movie-procurement policy, as well as to oppose the proposed United Nations Covenant of Human Rights. So outspoken is this midwestern Dies committee that local residents are somewhat reluctant, if not actually afraid, to oppose it publicly.

During the summer of 1950, the Americanism committee turned its suspicious eye on several movies which were being made available to the general public on a loan basis by the Peoria Public Library. . . . The particular movies under scrutiny by the Legion were three: *Brotherhood of Man, Boundary Lines,* and *Peoples of the USSR.* . . . All were made during or shortly after the war. In the Legion's opinion, each picture contained Communist propaganda. Therefore, said these Americanists, they should be withdrawn from circulation so that they could not pollute the minds of other Americans who were not subtle enough to distinguish the propaganda. . . .

[8] From "The Legion and the Library," by Loren P. Beth, assistant professor of political science, Bradley University, Peoria, Illinois. *New Republic.* 127:11-13. July 14, 1952. Reprinted by permission.

Should the films be withdrawn, if they do contain propaganda? This poses an important question of library policy, for if propaganda movies can be proscribed, logical extension could easily lead to equal proscription of books. Thus the whole policy of a library would become involved in the metaphysical and impossible task of screening every book, magazine or movie to see whether or not it contains Communist propaganda.

We also have here in an obvious if covert form the vital question, What *is* Communist propaganda? *In Brotherhood of Man,* the only thing this reviewer could find that sounded communistic was the advocacy of racial brotherhood; but racial brotherhood, as an ideal, was proposed quite some time before the Communist party was born. Obviously, the thought process which leads to the pillaging of an idea just because Communists espouse it can be carried to extreme lengths. Marx, after all, was in favor of public schools. It would be difficult, if not impossible, if movies were to be culled for subversive propaganda, for the censor to avoid using his own personal conceptions of good and bad as a guide. . . .

The outcome of the preliminary skirmishes was the withdrawal of the films from "general" circulation. Special rules were set up under which only groups legitimately "studying propaganda" would be permitted to view them. . . .

The battle over the three movies, however, was not yet over. The second round came in connection with a fourth film, the United Nations' production, *Of Human Rights,* which advocates the universal adoption of a Bill of Rights. . . .

The critical point here is that the Legion again demanded the withdrawal of this frankly propagandistic film on the grounds that it showed violations of human rights in this country but not in Russia.

At about this time another local pressure group entered the picture, this time on the opposite side. Many Peoria ministers had viewed the campaign against the first three movies with misgivings. Several had spoken in favor of the films on grounds that they were not propagandistic; a few had opposed any censorship regardless of the propaganda issue. . . . Eventually, the Peoria Ministerial Association passed, by a large majority, a resolution firmly opposing any sort of censorship and strongly backing the librarian.

Such pressure from the liberal side encouraged the library board; it was further emboldened by the fact that the attack on the UN movie was not nearly as successful in arousing the public as the earlier campaign had been. Consequently, the board rescinded its partial ban on the first films, and all four are now in general circulation. However, every new movie the library purchases which, in the opinion of the librarian, is "controversial," is to be previewed before a group of leading citizens representing local civic organizations. Then the movie will be released, with the written comments of the reviewer attached to the film can. Administratively, this may prove to be a difficult business: but it has a more serious objection, which is that, like the Communist party, the American Legion is vigilant, intolerant and energetic in applying pressure against all who challenge its views. . . .

The deeper implications of the library campaign, however, are not restricted to Peoria. They involve basic questions of policy for public libraries the country over. Should they refrain from buying "controversial" films in order to avoid the same troubles that have beset the Peoria institution? Most librarians will be very reluctant to shoulder personally the responsibility for defending the educational and informational tasks which are basic to the existence of the public-library system. The result may well be that these libraries will feel free to show only those movies which favor nothing; because espousal of any cause may offend some group.

Even were one to accept the idea of some sort of censorship for library films, however, one would still be faced with the important considerations of who will be the censor and under what restrictions. What the Legion committee ostensibly desires is a new librarian who will apply its concepts of Americanism. But even if such a librarian could be found, it is questionable whether librarians serving the entire community should be hired and fired, or forced to cater to, the behests of a small group of self-styled patriots. . . .

Too many men will share the Legion's prejudices in the mistaken belief that they are acting as conservatives should. They are in fact storing up troubles for themselves in years in which conservatism may hold the place of unpopularity that suspected radicalism holds today. As Justice Holmes saw so clearly, freedom for the thought that we hate is more important to democracy than freedom for the thoughts we like.

SOLUTION OF THE PEORIA CASE [9]

As the author of the motion which set up the plan the [Peoria] library is now using, I am more than a little interested in Mr. Beth's comments on it. . . . The motion . . . provides that previews shall be held for all films on national, international, political, economic, social and religious subjects. . . . Since the library sent out invitations for the one and only preview yet necessary to between five and six hundred civic organizations, the previewers sent by those groups which chose to participate constituted a good cross-section of American citizens.

It was thought that this method gave all interested groups opportunity to publicize their opinions and that the film users might accept or reject these or formulate new views of their own. . . . The practice of attaching the comments [of previewers] to the film-can, intended as a convenience for users who might wish to read them, created considerable difficulty of a mechanical or physical nature. . . . Consequently at a recent meeting the board approved the use of folders for the comment sheets. These folders are now offered to film users when the film is checked out. Borrowers may or may not accept the collection of comments, as they please. The films, which were once restricted, are now in unrestricted circulation. The librarian purchases whatever films he sees fit, for previews and opportunity for comment come only after purchase.

[9] From "Pressures on Peoria," reply to "The Legion and the Library," by Hazel C. Wolf, member of the Peoria Library Board. *New Republic.* 127:2-4. August 11, 1952. Reprinted by permission.

A POLICY OF LIMITED CIRCULATION [10]

A war of new dimensions is being fought today. To land, sea and the air has been added a fourth battleground, the minds of men. So important has this become that entire countries have been taken over without the firing of a single shot. . . . In such a time of crisis what do we who bear the responsibility for shaping the character of service in public libraries really believe that role to be? . . .

It is inevitable that long years of thinking and professional discussion on this activity should have evolved a code of principles which is deep seated; namely "That there should be the fullest practicable provision of material presenting all points of view concerning the problems and issues of our times, international, national and local." The usual interpretation of this—no censorship of reading materials—keeps open important channels for one of the enemy's important weapons of warfare, propaganda. For months I have thought of the incompatibility of this library policy with my obligation as an American citizen and with the obligation of the institution I represent which is a part of the government itself. . . .

Justice Oliver Wendell Holmes in a much quoted opinion has very pertinent things to say regarding freedom of speech:

> The most stringent protection of free speech would not protect a man in falsely shouting fire in a theatre and causing a panic. . . . The question in every case is whether the words used are used in such circumstances and are of such a nature as to create a clear and present danger that they will bring about the substantive evils that Congress has a right to prevent.

In Detroit after months of discussion the Library Commission . . . [adopted] a brief statement of book selection policies defined in terms of service objectives. . . . The statement in part follows:

> The Home Reading services provide the books for general nonspecialized readers, then through stimulation and guidance promote their

[10] From "Book Selection Policies," an address by Ralph A. Ulveling, director, Detroit Public Library, and past president of the American Library Association, at Illinois Summer Education Conference, Chicago, June 26, 1951. *Library Journal.* 76:1170-1. August 1951. Reprinted by permission.

use, to the end that children, young people, men and women, may have opportunity and encouragement for their fullest development as individuals, as members of a family, as citizens. Since this service is concerned with the best personal development of people through existing knowledge, rather than with the refinement and extension of knowldge itself, its purpose in selecting books is to choose the most usable that are available at varying levels, without regard to any obligations the total institution may have for preserving knowledge in its most comprehensive sense, or for maintaining open avenues for the fullest exercise of intellectual freedom of inquiry.

The Reference-Research services provide the usual as well as the obscure, the scholarly, and even the socially, economically, religiously or politically unorthodox materials necessary for research, for freedom of inquiry, and for information of all types.

Operating under this document, sound factual information on communism would be proper inclusions in both services; Communist expressions of opinion or misleading propaganda would be found in only the Reference service where duplication of titles is limited. Thus people with inquiring minds or study needs will have full scope for their investigations while the general readers will have placed before them only the books which have been chosen because of their importance in helping people to realize their best development and to carry out their obligations ably and well. The implications of this distinction in so far as it may have application to smaller libraries which cannot on their more limited budgets be "all things to all men" I leave to your decision.

PLEA FOR CALM JUDGMENT [11]

He [Mr. Ulveling] says that the first clause in paragraph two of the Library Bill of Rights, as usually interpreted, leaves open important channels for enemy propaganda, and that the noncensorship it implies is incompatible with his duty as an American. . . .

There *is* danger that Americans will be deceived into destroying their rights, but not (now) by Communist propaganda. In fact, the very rights with which librarians are most concerned,

[11] From "Keep Calm and Support the Library Bill of Rights," by Thurston Taylor, librarian, Free Public Library, Worcester, Massachusetts. *Library Journal.* 77:2063-4. December 15, 1951. Reprinted by permission.

freedom of speech and of the press, are being threatened from the other side. . . .

Our libraries are certainly filled with anti-Communist expressions of opinion and propaganda, some of it misleading. There can be little doubt that today it bulks many times larger than official Communist propaganda, which is certainly found in very small quantities in even our largest libraries. Librarians need to be aware of both and to handle both (especially the Communist) with tact and discrimination. But surely librarians don't need to be warned to put it out of sight! They will be too ready to do that anyway, if indeed they are aware of its existence.

It is inconceivable that Mr. Ulveling would have us identify as Communist, material from various sources more or less liberal or more or less left, which may agree to a greater or less extent with the "Communist line." . . .

Yet, if Mr. Ulveling does not mean that it is the librarian's duty to "protect" readers from extreme and intemperate opinion, what does he mean? If he means to propose a change in the Library Bill of Rights, he does not put into words the change that he himself would accept. . . .

It is a good thing that the Library Bill of Rights was adopted in 1948, before the fear of communism reached its present stage of intensity. But if it is to accomplish its purpose of helping to protect the library's special role in any fight for freedom, we cannot begin to tamper with it now; on the contrary we will certainly have to close ranks and defend it against attacks much more dangerous than any that have yet appeared. . . .

Our greatest enemy is our own fear and panic—fear of Communists, fear of anti-Communists, fear of smear. . . . Librarians should be able to keep calm and a little detached from the extremes of opinion.

DON'T SPLIT COLLECTIONS [12]

Whatever the value of Mr. Ulveling's statement for the Detroit Public or other large libraries, it cannot be applied successfully to small or medium-sized libraries without destroying

[12]From an article by Paul Bixler, secretary, Committee on Intellectual Freedom, American Library Association, and librarian, Antioch College, Yellow Springs, Ohio. *Library Journal.* 76:2064-5. December 15, 1951. Reprinted by permission.

their usefulness as distributors of ideas. . . . By far the greater number of libraries in the United States cannot easily divide their collections and their facilities into two parts as one would divide the Red Sea. . . .

Let us suppose, however, that a medium-sized or a small library does accomplish this job of separation. What has taken place? First of all, a kind of general labeling. This group of books, it has been decided, are so "important" that they must be segregated behind the desk or in closed stacks. This other group is not so "important" and may be freely examined and taken out of the library. . . .

Such a change would be a revolution, and a disastrous one. For it would eat away one of the principal advantages and values of the medium and small library—whatever is inherently useful and significant in the open-shelf system. The advantage and the value are not easily articulated, but they have great significance for the library client who is beginning to find his way among ideas. . . .

The new plan would seriously disturb the library's development in the field of adult education. Here the library client comes most vitally in contact with and learns to handle ideas. But ideas are neither born nor do they live in a vacuum. They must be dramatized, compared, and allowed to struggle in combat with one another. If, then, there is restriction in the statement of such ideas, as seems to be contemplated here . . . in the end the discussion of ideas will be restricted and adult education will be a limited and perhaps a dying affair. . . .

There are no men in the American library system for whom I have more respect and liking than Mr. Ulveling. But I must depart from his analysis of the war ideas. . . . "So important has this become [he says] that entire countries have been taken over without the firing of a single shot." This statement is quite misleading, for it implies that the Communists have won at least occasionally without the use of force. And that is simply not true. In Czechoslovakia—the classic example of victory without bloodshed—Soviet guns were on the border. Moreover, the Czech Communists were a minority; in fact, it is now the best opinion that they moved when they did because they were losing the battle for men's minds in Czechoslovakia.

How do you fight a war for men's minds? Well, we don't know all the answers to that one. But we do know that you don't fight it by imitating the censoring, repressive tactics of the enemy. If those were the weapons, we would inevitably lose. For we have no practice in them. Whereas censorship and police control are two inventions the Soviets know so well that they can justly lay claim to all the most up-to-date patents.

This is a war for the world. And our ignorance of the world is so great that we need every scrap of information, opinion, and debate that we can stimulate. We do not sufficiently recognize that we have already won the first battle in this intellectual war—a battle fought right here at home. Two years ago the chief public issue was individual economic well-being and comfort. Today by overwhelming evidence in the public polls it is American foreign policy. That is evidence of a great victory. And it was won not by repression, censorship, or the segregation of fact and opinion, but by ferocious public drive and debate—and yes, even by hysteria and in the face of slander.

Can we take this kind of war indefinitely? Nobody knows for certain. But if we think we can't, we might better fold up now and give the world over to the Communists. Outside this country we are only beginning to fight the war for the minds of men. We have much to learn. We won't learn it by being completely cautious, by putting the words of Lenin, Marx, Stalin, and William Foster out of sight in a locked case, or simply by talking to ourselves about democracy.

SEGREGATION OF QUESTIONABLE MATERIAL [13]

"There should be the fullest practicable provision of material presenting all points of view . . ." so says the Library Bill of Rights. We would have little interest today in discussing this trite statement, reflecting as it does nothing more than long established library policy and practice, if it were not for the

[13] From "The Large Public Library," by Ralph Munn, Director of Carnegie Library, Pittsburgh, and past president of the American Library Association. In *Freedom of Communication;* proceedings of the First Conference on Intellectual Freedom, New York City, June 28-29, 1952; edited by William Dix and Paul Bixler. American Library Association. Chicago. 1954. p. 44-9. Reprinted by permission.

Russian imperialist brand of communism as exemplified in the cold war. It is the threat of this force which gives importance to the bill, and urgency to our discussions.

Let us then discover the types of materials relating to Russia and communism which are involved:

1. There are official expositions of communism as expressed by Marx and Engels, and developed by Lenin, Stalin and others. These are historic documents relating to the founding and development of ideas which are shaking the world. Unquestionably, they are proper source material for the public library.

2. Biographies of the founders and developers of communism should be collected just as they are in the fields of religion, education, science or any other world force.

3. Histories of Russia, including the Soviet era, and those written by Russians or written from their point of view, should be provided.

4. Factual explanations of the Soviet system of government by recognized writers of any country, including Russia, are clearly a proper library resource.

5. Such official Russian documents as are available, and unofficial yearbooks and statistical manuals are necessary reference sources.

6. Popular books covering the current scene present more problems, but the ordinary standards concerning the authority and objectivity of the author are the main guides in selection. Even the best of these books will bring some complaints from those people who object to acknowledgment of any Soviet accomplishment; to write that the Soviets have made any advances in education, science or industry is treasonable to them. We must, of course, take a firm stand against these objectors.

Included in the current books are some items of disguised Russian propaganda. As citizens and librarians we should recognize that propaganda has become a vital weapon of warfare. Its purposes are to instill doubts, cause dissension and strife within a nation, and finally to undermine purpose and morale to such a degree that defense is no longer possible. Surely this knowledge places certain positive obligations upon the librarian. Among these obligations is that of attempting to identify items of disguised propaganda and eliminating them from the library's general collection. Written by people who may not be known to be Communist sympathizers, cleverly presented to avoid open adherence to the Communist line by subtly supporting it, these books are, of course, deliberately deceptive. (Author's note: A review by Edgar Ansel Mowrer in the March 15, 1952, issue of the *Saturday Review*, v35, no 11, p 18, tells how to write a pro-Communist book without seeming to do so.)

I am not one of those librarians who strain to explain any act of censorship as a routine aspect of book selection. To my mind, however, the rejection of disguised propaganda is fully covered by one of the traditional tenets of selection—that a book shall be honest, that it shall be what it purports to be. Except for the occasional literary hoax, we do not knowingly select books which were written for the express purpose of deceiving our readers. Call it book selection or censorship, as you will, I believe it to be our duty to try to discover—and I know we cannot catch it all—and to eliminate disguised propaganda from the general collection. Some libraries may wish to form a special collection of these propaganda items; study of the technique of propaganda is, of course, important in itself.

7. Finally we come to open propaganda, such as the *Daily Worker, Masses and Mainstream, New World Review,* and books by . . . avowed Communists. Here there is no attempt at deception. The publication does not pretend to be one thing when it is in fact quite another. Those who use open propaganda know, or should know, its source and nature. Most of its users do so for a specific purpose. Many items of open propaganda should, I am sure, be collected and preserved.

With the decision to try to identify and eliminate disguised propaganda from the general collection, there remains the problem of determining the treatment of the other groups of materials. Where and under what conditions shall they be shelved?

Most laws contain at least one vital word which is subject to varying interpretations. If this were not so, our attorneys would starve to death. So it is with the Library Bill of Rights where we find the word "provision"—to repeat: "There should be the fullest practicable provision of material presenting all points of view. . . ." What does "provision" mean?

There are three generally accepted ways in which a public library can make provision of materials. First, materials can be placed on open shelves in the reading rooms, or, in some of the newer buildings, in adjacent open stacks. Second, materials can be placed in storage stacks which are not open to the public but from which materials are available simply by filing an unsigned call slip in a completely impersonal and routine way. Third, by consigning materials to a restricted section from which they can be secured only by personal application to a librarian. If the library elects to collect Communist propaganda as such, it should either be placed in a restricted section, or—and here comes the naughty word—it should be labeled as propaganda. All of the other categories of materials which I have listed should, I think, be readily available on open shelves or in the stacks.

There is room, I am sure, for honest differences of opinion among well-meaning persons concerning the open display of books which can be regarded as having subversive features. My own thinking is strongly influenced by the fact that when we display a book we are inviting its use by people who have never heard of it. In the case of *New World Review,* for example, we are actually becoming a part of the Russian propaganda machine if we display it; we are in effect, becoming a recruiting agent for Russia and communism. If placed in the stacks, this same material is readily available to any person who knows of the publication, or who uses the subject catalog. This, to my mind, is making an adequate provision of materials under the Library Bill of Rights.

Branch libraries are seldom equipped with storage stacks, and the only choice may lie between the reading room shelves and a restricted section, often the librarian's office. Because of the limited physical facilities of branch buildings, it is a long standing practice to eliminate certain items from their collections. Treatises on sex, novels not suited for general circulation, and small expensive technical handbooks are examples. I would frankly include some of these propaganda items as unsuited to the limited facilities of a branch. Most of these materials are, of course, available to the branch user through the regular delivery service from Central. Here, again, I believe this to be an adequate provision. Also, I am sure that it is possible to select materials for the open shelves which do cover all sides of current questions, including the Russian viewpoint, without hidden or objectionable propaganda.

DISCUSSION OF SEGREGATION [14]

[In the discussion following Mr. Munn's talk, the following exchanges took place.—Ed.]

A number of questions were asked of Mr. Munn concerning 'disguised propaganda." Who, for example, was to determine what was disguised propaganda? Mr. Munn pointed out that some years back most of the disguised propaganda came to libraries in the form of pamphlets "supposedly published by super-duper Americanism groups which deliberately adopted those names to throw us off the scent." As to current disguised propaganda, "all you can do is to get all the possible information from reviews, from committees, newspapers," discovering "who these people are and their connections as far as you can." The decision, he said, "will have to be made within the library, of course . . . presumably by a staff committee with the participation of the librarian."

"Good" propaganda, someone pointed out, could be supported with facts, "bad" propaganda could not be so supported; and the difficulty with propaganda from the Soviet Union was that one could not go behind the Iron Curtain to check on the facts. Mr. Munn commented that the problem presented by Russian propaganda was a difficult one. Admittedly we would make mistakes in handling it but he believed we had "the obligation to do the best we can."

Mr. Cushman [the speaker quoted in the article immediately following] commented that both the Communist party and the American Legion as well as other groups contend that they

[14] From "Summary of Discussion." In *Freedom of Communication*; proceedings of the First Conference on Intellectual Freedom, New York City, June 28-29, 1952; edited by William Dix and Paul Bixler. American Library Association. Chicago. 1954. p64-9. Reprinted by permission.

follow the highest principles of Americanism. We must not simply fall for terminology, he said; we can best put our own Americanism into practice by following out our professional principles of book selection. . . .

There was further disagreement with Mr. Munn over placing certain materials in restricted areas.

Mr. Munn: I want to make it very plain that the only type of literature which I said should be restricted is that type of literature which is written for propaganda reasons only, and that it should constitute a special collection which should be held for those who are especially interested, particularly those university classes which are making a special study of the techniques of propaganda itself. . . .

Mr. Cushman: Mr. Munn, the National Association of Manufacturers also puts out what the AFL says is propaganda. Therein lies the crux of our situation, it seems to me.

From the audience came a question about the definition of propaganda.

Mr. Munn: I don't have a definition in mind. I think you know and I know what we have in mind, namely that sort of material which is written with something between the lines, the innuendo which makes it something which is not apparent on the surface, on the first reading—something that is put there deliberately in order to impress or deceive the reader. That's somewhere near it, isn't it?

CITADELS OF FREE COMMUNICATION [15]

The line of demarcation between acceptability and nonacceptability of books for library use is becoming less and less clear. It is not that the principles of book selection have materially changed but rather that the irrationalities of the present period of social, economic and political upheaval are forcing different emphases upon its application. The problem is pointed up by

[15] From "The Small Public Library," by Jerome Cushman, librarian, Salina (Kansas) Public Library. In *Freedom of Communication;* proceedings of the First Conference on Intellectual Freedom, New York City, June 28-29, 1952; edited by William Dix and Paul Bixler. American Library Association. Chicago. 1954. p50-4. Reprinted by permission.

the confusions and alarms raised by those who would "stereotype belief into persecution." Another factor also symptomatic of our times is unvarnished fear, the type that results in silence when active commitment is required. Librarians and their boards of trustees have become extra-sensitive to pressures both in and outside the community regarding books which are considered dangerous for reader consumption by individuals or groups.

The small public library has a special vulnerability to these pressures. Because of the personal and individual aspects of its service, due in great measure to the size of the city [the population of Salina is 26,000] and the fact that the librarian is often more closely identified with the everyday workings of his institution, the small library finds itself in a more exposed position than the larger and more impersonal unit. . . . It is more apparent in a small institution that our primary emphasis is on books. And so, for us, books remain the focal point in interpreting the services of our library to the community. . . .

Formulation of criteria for book selection presents few difficulties. They are well known and are echoed in textbooks and staff manuals and by convention speakers. But when a well-meaning group seeks to formulate the library collection in its own image of truth, it seldom does good to cite the factors that influenced the decision for the purchase of the item. These critics are not interested in the virtues or faults of the books, but rather in what they think reading them will do to the unwary innocents who have not been forewarned. A librarian can run into trouble when he makes reviews the final criteria of book selection. Upon which review or reviews shall he depend? Shall his judgment of the book be based upon the numerical majority of reviews in favor of it? And what about the relative merit of reviews and reviewers? Is it a matter of which side of the fence the librarian is on, the liberal or conservative? These questions, if asked by an irate group, lead the librarian down an embarrassing blind alley. It can make him realize, if nothing else, that there are no absolutes in this business of book selection. Relying on authority is always a dangerous game because there is always someone who claims his authority has true validity. Reviews may serve the librarian as guideposts toward mature decisions in book selection, but cannot take the place of his basic responsibility to understand the function of communication and man in a free society.

It is not selection but rejection that is the hub of this problem. Robert Leigh [director of the Carnegie-sponsored Public Library Inquiry and author of *The Public Library in the United States*] found that most librarians were liberal in regard to their book selection practices. While his report was not made in today's atmosphere of hypertension, there is an indication that courage is not an unknown attribute among many of our colleagues. The librarian must meet the problem of rejecting books and still apply the principle of fairness to differing viewpoints. Here is how our library resolves this perplexity. If a book is rejected because it does not in our opinion fill a library need, we can be persuaded by a patron to either borrow or purchase the volume. We are not amenable to group pressure for the inclusion of books on our shelves which we do not feel belong, but we will allow them to purchase items for us which promulgate their particular brand of truth. Here is one concrete example. The report of the Commission on Freedom of the Press under the chairmanship of Robert H. Hutchins was purchased for the library. We did not stock *Freedom and the Press,* by Frank Hughes. However, we received two calls for the book and consequently purchased it. Thus due to patron requests we receive books that in our opinion do not add to the quality of our book collection. On the other hand, we are kept from the danger of the false assumption that our selections are always right and that we know what is best for the people. In other words, just as we cannot be influenced to ban books from our shelves, we can be influenced to place books upon them.

Every book in our library belongs on its regular shelf along with like books, unless there is an occasion for a special display. There are no books, in our opinion, that merit the special attention of being placed in the librarian's office or anywhere else that keeps them from being readily accessible to the public. We did have to replace a snappy volume on photographic modeling a couple of times, but we did not let this irresistible interest in things artistic upset our basic policy. Labeling books holds no charm for us and we very gently refused an offer to help us tag our volumes. Nor can we agree with a colleague who places in selected earthy novels the following notice, "This book is placed in the library because of public demand and does not reflect the buying policy." . . .

Before book selection policies are formed there are community considerations which a small public library might analyze. First and foremost, there must be a thorough understanding with the Board of Trustees resulting in their positive commitment to the Library Bill of Rights. This obviates, in the case of our library, the necessity for any other written set of book selection principles. The prestige and force of the library profession is behind the Library Bill of Rights, and it avoids the danger entailed in too much spelling-out. Secondly, there are men and women in every community from a newspaper editor to a doctor's wife who may be depended upon to resist threats to a free public library. The librarian would do well to know these people so that their power can be added to the "stubborn ounces of weight" exerted by the library in any question of freedom from censorship.

We must be alert to the forces that would destroy the library's function as a free institution. Still we must not overestimate our importance. Many of the foundation-shaking battles that we wage with the forces of reaction hardly make a ripple in the consciousness of the community. By keeping perspective and realizing that it takes all kinds of Americans to make America, we stand a better chance of being regarded as a bulwark, meriting the confidence of all facets of opinion. The library must be, as Caesar's wife, blameless before all. In implementing its book selection policies it must, according to Dr. Leigh, identify itself as the one institution that is "technically best suited to be a chief citadel of free communication." If a segment of the community seeks to abrogate this point of view then the library must resist every pressure exerted upon it.

The librarian need not be afraid. He has on his side the impetus of a powerful tradition that has helped shape the modern world and is still a dynamic force in the realm of ideas. This tradition, stemming from the Judaic-Christian values, encompasses man's questioning spirit and will permit him to solve his own destiny. We need not fear the "one idea'd fanatics who want to make their petty standards the measure of our freedom." Ours is an era in which change has the inexorability of the tides. Man is expressing himself, and no authoritarian pattern, no status-quoism will prevent him from assuming responsibility for his future. It is for us librarians, conscious of our regard for man the individual, to keep open the lanes of free communication so that we can say with Archibald MacLeish, "The true test of freedom is in its use."

SELECTION VS. CENSORSHIP [16]

When librarians discuss the matter among themselves, they are quite satisfied with the distinction between censorship and selection and are in smug agreement that the librarian practices the latter, not the former. Non-librarians are less disposed to be so generous in their interpretation of the librarian's action. Thus in its article on censorship, the *Enclyclopaedia of the Social Sciences* points out that "libraries and booksellers have sometimes undertaken to censor books 'personally scandalous, libelous, immoral, or otherwise disagreeable,' " and Morris Ernst is even more outspoken:

The subterranean censorship may appear in the public library as well. . . . Do public libraries attempt to supervise the tastes of their readers by making it a fixed policy not to buy "objectionable" books? It is a simple expedient and has often been applied. The public librarian often has the plausible excuse that as the funds of a library are limited, he must pick and choose, and naturally the more "wholesome" books are to be preferred. He insists that he is exercising not censorship but the prerogative of free selection. Nevertheless, the character of this choice is often suspicious. [Ernst, M. L. and Seagle, William. *To the Pure; a Study of Obscenity and the Censor.* Viking Press. New York. 1928. p 101.]

Clearly, in these two quotations, any deliberate bar against free access to a book is designated "censorship," and it does not

[16] From "Not Censorship But Selection," address by Lester Asheim, dean and assistant professor, University of Chicago Graduate Library School, before the American Library Association's Second Conference on Intellectual Freedom, Whittier, California, June 1953. *Wilson Library Bulletin.* 28:63-8. September 1953.

matter that the control is enforced by the librarian rather than by a postal authority or a pressure group. Does the librarian really have any grounds for claiming that there *is* a difference?

Our concern, here, of course, is not with cases where the librarian is merely carrying out an obligation placed upon him by law. Where the decision is not his to make, we can hardly hold him responsible for that decision. Thus the library which does not stock a book which may not be passed through customs or which is punishable by law as pornographic will not be considered here. The real question of censorship vs. selection arises when the librarian, exercising his own judgment, decides against a book which has every legal right to representation on his shelves. In other words, we should not have been concerned with the librarian who refused to buy *Ulysses* for his library before 1933—but we do have an interest in his refusal after the courts cleared it for general circulation in the United States. . . .

In its practical results, what is the essential difference to the patron who cannot get *Ulysses* from the library because the customs office refused its admission to the United States, because the librarian decided not to buy it, or because a local pressure group forced its removal from the shelves? . . .

The first instance illustrates censorship in its purest and simplest form: a work is banned from the entire country by legal action. If this is the characteristic of censorship, then the librarian is not a censor, for he does not go to law to enforce his judgment—and he does not because he has no intention of denying access to the book through any channel but that of his own agency. He does not say (as the law says), "This book shall not be circulated." He says only, "*I* will not circulate it."

The third instance illustrates censorship in its impurest and most complex form: a work is banned from an entire community by the extra-legal pressure of a small segment of the community. Again, it is the scope of the ban which distinguishes the second and third instances: the librarian controls only the content of his own institution; the pressure group attempts to control the content of all institutions, whether under their jurisdiction or not.

But the allegedly limited span of the librarian's control is not a sufficient virtue to absolve him of any suspicion of censorship

action. The local pressure group, after all, is also limited in its
effectiveness. . . .

Librarians do not deny that rejection occurs, but they claim
that the ideal of absolute equality for all books is unattainable
even supposing it were desirable. To demand that all books be
equally accessible is to demand that all books occupy the same
place on the same shelf—a physical impossibility. And as soon
as we defer to the laws of physics and place each book in a
different place, we shall start having some books less accessible
than others and shall be—in a sense—discriminating against the
least accessible.

But let us suppose that we recognize that equal accessibility is
unattainable, why should not all books be available at least?
Again we run into physical impossibility—no library in the world
is large enough to house even one copy of every printed publication. Nor is the difficulty merely physical, as any practicing
librarian knows from bitter experience. Long before we are
allowed to test the physical limits of complete availability we are
brought up short by financial limits. . . . So complete representation of every title ever published is an idle dream. Consequently
some titles will not be purchased, and that is rejection.

Many librarians would say that, in such a situation, that is
also selection, and they would like to stop the discussion at that
point. . . . It would be dishonest to pretend, however, that
financial considerations are the only ones which shape the
judgment to purchase or reject. The librarian also feels an
obligation to select in terms of standards—and there are some
books that he would not buy, even if money were not a
problem. . . .

One of our standards, for example, is the presumed intent
of the author and the sincerity of his purpose. . . . When a book
attacks a basic belief or a way of life to which we are emotionally
attached, its purpose will seem to us to be vicious rather than
constructive; dangerous rather than valuable; deserving of suppression rather than of widespread dissemination. . . .

Literary excellence is a second criterion to which most
librarians would subscribe, but again the judgments are essentially
subjective . . . A reader who does not like a book usually con-

siders it to be badly written; conversely a book whose ideas please him will seem to be one which is written well. . . .

Still another criterion for selection is the presumed effect upon the reader, and here again we have only our guesses, based upon our own individual and subjective reaction. . . .

Lastly, librarians agree with the courts that the time, and the customs of the community, are important elements to be considered in judging the value and effectiveness of a book. Such a standard, however, is a strong support for a censorship which would stultify the development of a literature and the propagation of thought and ideas. Almost all of the great classics have been books which said something new, or said something differently, ahead of or not in step with the custom and traditions of the community. . . .

If we are agreed that the standards employed as touchstones by the librarians are essentially the same as those used by the censor, the distinction between selection and censorship will have to be found in the way the standards are applied. . . .

The major characteristic which makes for the all-important difference seems to me to be this: that the selector's approach is positive, while that of the censor is negative. This is more than a verbal quibble; it transforms the entire act and the steps included in it. For to the selector, the important thing is to find reasons to keep the book. . . . For the censor, on the other hand, the important thing is to find reasons to reject the book; his guiding principle leads him to seek out the objectionable features, the weaknesses, the possibilities for misinterpretation. The positive selector asks what the reaction of a rational intelligent adult would be to the content of the work; the censor fears for the results on the weak, the warped, and the irrational. The selector says, if there is anything good in this book let us try to keep it; the censor says, if there is anything bad in this book, let us reject it. And since there is seldom a flawless work in any form, the censor's approach can destroy much that is worth saving.

An inevitable consequence of the negative approach is that it leads to the use of isolated parts rather than the complete whole upon which to base a judgment. Taken out of context and given a weight completely out of keeping with their place in the over-all work, single words and unrelated passages can be used to damn a book. This technique has been typical of many of the most notorious instances of censorship: the major theme, the total purpose, the effect of the work as a unified whole have been ignored in order to focus on a word or phrase or sequence. . . .

The librarian, if he is truly a selector and not a censor, does not succumb to irrelevancies—introduced either by the prejudices of his own background or the pressures of his library's patrons. He admits the right of the reader to take issue with the writer, but he is swayed by arguments only where they have relevance to the book itself, and to the book as a whole. . . .

Finally, the selector begins, ideally, with a presumption in favor of liberty of thought; the censor does not. The aim of the selector is to promote reading, not to inhibit it; to multiply the points of view which will find expression, not limit them; to be a channel for communication, not a bar against it. . . .

Selection, then, begins with a presumption in favor of liberty of thought; censorship, with a presumption in favor of thought control. Selection's approach to the book is positive, seeking its values in the book as a book, and in the book as a whole. Censorship's approach is negative, seeking for vulnerable characteristics wherever they can be found—anywhere within the book, or even outside it. Selection seeks to protect the right of the reader to read; censorship seeks to protect—not the right—but the reader himself from the fancied effects of his reading. The selector has faith in the intelligence of the reader; the censor has faith only in his own.

BIBLIOGRAPHY

An asterisk (*) preceding a reference indicates that the article or a part of it has been reprinted in this book.

BIBLIOGRAPHIES

BOOKS, PAMPHLETS, AND DOCUMENTS

*Alabama. House of Representatives. Act No.888, H.644: An act relating to schools, to prohibit the use of certain textbooks and writings in public schools, institutions of higher learning, and trade schools, approved September 19, 1953.
> *Same.* 1 p. mimeo. American Textbook Publishers Institute. 1 Madison Ave. New York 10. '53.

Allen, F. L. Big change. 308p. Harper & Bros. New York. '52.

American Book Publishers Council. Books and our constitutional guarantees. 5p. mimeo. The Council. 2 W. 46th St. New York 36. '53.

American Book Publishers Council. Recent censorship developments. 6p. mimeo. The Council. 2 W. 46th St. New York 36. '53.

American Book Publishers Council. Recent developments in the censorship field. 6p. mimeo. The Council. 2 W. 46th St. New York 36. '53.

American Book Publishers Council. Recent pressures on books. 12p. mimeo. The Council. 2 W. 46th St. New York 36. '53.

*American Book Publishers Council. Review of major developments in state legislatures (January-July, 1953). The Council. 2 W. 46th St. New York 36. Ag. '53.

American Book Publishers Council. Summary of Federal Judge Charles J. McNamee's decision in Youngstown, Ohio, suit filed by New American Library. The Council. 2 W. 46th St. New York 36. '52.

*American Civil Liberties Union. Policy statement on pressure-group censorship. 6p. mimeo. The Union. 170 Fifth Ave. New York 10. '52.

American Legion. Department of Michigan. Evaluation of instructional materials; statement adopted at convention, Grand Rapids, Mich., August 19-22, 1948. 3p. mimeo. The Legion. 602 Barlum Tower. Detroit 26, Mich. '48.
> *Same.* 3p. mimeo. American Textbook Publishers Institute. New York. '48.

American Library Association. Committee on Intellectual Freedom. Newsletter on intellectual freedom. mimeo. The Committee. Antioch College Library. Yellow Springs, Ohio.
> Newsletters dated Je., Ag., S.-O., N. '52; Ja., F., My., O. '53.

American Textbook Publishers Institute. American way of publishing—your safeguard against subversion in textbooks. 8p. The Institute. 1 Madison Ave. New York 10. '53.

American Textbook Publishers Institute. Attack on textbooks. 2p. The Institute. 1 Madison Ave. New York 10. '51.

    Same. Ohio Schools. 30:352-3. N. '52; *Same.* Texas Outlook. 37: 14-17. Mr. '53; *Same.* Wisconsin Journal of Education. 85:15-18. D. '52; *Same condensed.* Education Digest. 18:1-4. N. '52.

Barnes, H. E. Struggle against the historical blackout. 87p. The author. Stonewood. Cooperstown, N.Y. '53.

Bernays, E. L. Safeguarding civil liberties today. 158p. Cornell University Press. Ithaca, N.Y. '45.

Biddle, F. B. Fear of freedom. 263p. Doubleday & Co. New York. '51.

*Burke, R. A. What is the index? 129p. Bruce Publishing Company. Milwaukee, Wis. '52.

Casey, R. D.; Smith, B. L.; Laswell, H. D. Propaganda, communication and public opinion. 445p. Princeton University Press. Princeton, N.J. '46.

Chafee, Zechariah. Free speech in the United States. 634p. Harvard University Press. Cambridge, Mass. '41.

The Christophers. Your right to object. 32p. The authors. 18 E. 48th St. New York 17. '54.

Commager, H. S. Freedom, loyalty, dissent. 155p. Oxford University Press. New York. '54.

*Conference on Intellectual Freedom. Freedom of communication; proceedings of the first conference, New York City, June 28-29, 1952; William Dix and Paul Bixler, eds. 143p. American Library Association. Chicago. '54.

Cooke, Alistair. Generation on trial. 842p. Alfred A. Knopf, Inc. New York. '50.

Craig, Alec. Above all liberties. 205p. W. W. Norton & Co. New York. '42.

Ernst, M. L. First freedom. 316p. Macmillan Co. New York. '46.

Ernst, M. L. and Linley, Alexander. Censor marches on. 346p. Doubleday, Doran & Co. New York. '40.

Ernst, M. L. and Seagle, William. To the pure; a study of obscenity and the censor. 336p. Viking Press. New York. '28.

Federal supplement, cases argued and determined in the District Courts of the United States and the Court of Claims. v 1-. West Publishing Co. St. Paul, Minn. '33-.

    United States v. One Book Called "Ulysses." v5, Federal supplement, 182, 194. United States District Court. Southern District of N.Y. '33.

*Hance, M. G. Report on our San Antonio public libraries, Communist front authors and their books therein. 15p. mimeo. The Author. 230 Overhill Drive. San Antonio, Tex. '53.

Hulburd, David. This happened in Pasadena. 106p. Macmillan Co. New York. '51.

John Dewey Society. Eleventh Year Book: Education for a world society. 273p. Harper & Bros. New York. '51.

Jones, H. M. Primer of intellectual freedom. 191p. Harvard University Press. Cambridge, Mass. '49.

*Lacy, Dan. Freedom and books; address to Georgia State Library Association, St. Simons Island, October 24, 1953. 12p. mimeo. American Book Publishers Council. 2 W. 46th St. New York 36. '53.

Leigh, R. D. Public Library in the United States. 272p. Columbia University Press. New York 27. '50.

Lyons, Eugene. Red decade. 423p. Bobbs-Merrill. Indianapolis, Ind. '41.

McWilliams, Carey. Witch hunt. 361p. Little, Brown & Co. Boston. '50.

*Malin, P. M. Testimony before Gathings Special Committee on Current Pornographic Materials. 6p. mimeo. American Civil Liberties Union. 170 Fifth Ave. New York 10.

Meiklejohn, Alexander. Free speech and its relation to government. 107p. Harper & Bros. New York. '48.

*Mill, J. S. On liberty; representative government; the subjection of women. 548p. Oxford University Press. London. '33.
  Excerpts from essay "On liberty" (p5-141) are reprinted in this book.

Milton, John. Areopagitica, and other prose works. (Everyman's Library) 306p. E. P. Dutton and Co. New York. '27.

*National Council of Teachers of English. Censorship and controversy; report of committee on censorship of teaching materials for classroom and library. 56p. The Council. 8110 S. Halsted St. Chicago 20. '53.

National Education Association. Education for international understanding in American schools. 241p. The Association. 1201 16th St., N.W. Washington 6, D.C. '48.

National Education Association. Platform and resolutions adopted at annual convention, Miami Beach, Fla., July, 1953. 3p. The Association. 1201 16th St., N.W. Washington 6, D.C. '53.

National Education Association. Commission for Defense of Democracy Through Education. Public school and the American heritage. 3p. The Association. 1201 16th St., N.W. Washington 6, D.C. '50.

National Education Association. Educational Policies Commission. UNESCO and American schools. 8p. The Commission. 1201 16th St., N.W. Washington 6, D.C. '52.

National Republic. Lettergram no249. Red pattern of penetration of education. 4p. National Republic Publishing Co. 511 11th St., N.W. Washington 4, D.C. '53.

New World Writing. 3d Mentor Selection. 360p. New American Library. New York. '53.
  Mead, Margaret. Sex and censorship in modern society. p7-24.

*New York University. Conference on Social Meaning of Legal Concepts. Social meaning of legal concepts; no5, Protection of public morals through censorship; Bernard Schwartz, ed. 88p. New York University. School of Law. 108 Washington Sq. E. New York 3. '53.

*Newsweek Club and Educational Bureaus. Censorship for the mass audience: a protection or a threat? (Platform study guide) 23p. The Bureaus. 152 W. 42d St. New York 18. '53.

Shores, L. S. ed. Challenges to librarianship. (Florida State University studies no 12) 156p. Florida State University Press. Tallahassee, Fla. '53.
    Evans, Luther. Challenge of censorship. p39-54.

Stevenson, Adlai. Speeches. 128p. Random House. New York. '52.
    Address before American Legion convention, New York, August 29, 1952. p82-3.

Texas. House of Representatives. H.B. No.566, March 10, 1952. An act making it unlawful to use or keep or allow to be used or kept in any public school or State-supported institution of higher learning certain types of books or other publications or literature which seek to discredit or reflect on the American form of government or way of life, or which are written by persons with Communist or subversive connections or background and are not so identified by certain printing and labeling; providing for complaints, investigations, determinations, orders, penalties, and forfeitures in connection with violations; and declaring an emergency. 3p. Austin, Tex. '52.

United Nations Educational, Scientific and Cultural Organization. Handbook for the improvement of textbooks and teaching materials as aids to international understanding. (Publication no368) 172p. Columbia University Press, New York 27. '49.

United States. Department of State. United Nations conference on freedom of information, Geneva, March 23-April 21, 1948, report of United States delegates with related documents. (Publication 3150) 45p. Division of Publications. Office of Public Affairs. Washington, D.C. '48.

United States. House of Representatives. Committee on Un-American Activities. Review of the Scientific and Cultural Conference for World Peace, arranged by the National Council of the Arts, Sciences and Professions and held in New York City March 25, 26 and 27, 1949. 58p. Supt. of Docs. Washington 25, D.C. '49.

*United States. House of Representatives. Select Committee on Current Pornographic Materials. Report. 137p. 82d Congress, 1st session. Supt. of Docs. Washington 25, D.C. '52.
    Reprinted in this book: Testimony of Rev. T. J. Fitzgerald, December 2, 1952, p47; testimony of H. W. Case, December 2, 1952, p50-63; recommendations by committee majority, p 116-20; address by Samuel Black before Atlantic Coast Independent Distributors, Hollywood Beach, Fla., April 25, 1952, p 131-4.

*United States. National Archives and Records Service. Federal Register Division. United States Government organization manual 1952-53; revised as of July 1, 1952. 742p. Supt. of Docs. Washington 25, D.C.
    First Amendment, Constitution of the United States.

*United States. Senate. Committee on Government Operation. Report on hearings before permanent subcommittee on investigations. 83d Congress, 1st session. Supt. of Docs. Washington 25, D.C. '53.
    Reprinted in this book: Excerpts from testimony of L. F. Budenz, March 25, 1953 (pt 1, p41-59).

Van Doren, Mark. Man's right to knowledge and the free use thereof; Columbia University bicentennial brochure. 106p. Columbia University Press. New York. '54.

Veterans of Foreign Wars. Colonel Frank Brezina Post. Address by F. F. Lyons, Nov. 15, 1952. 15p. The Post. Box 702. Encinitas, Cal. '52.

Young, E. J. Looking behind the censorships. 368p. J. B. Lippincott Co. Philadelphia. '38.

PERIODICALS

*America. 88:611. Mr. 7, '53. Right to object against smut; editorial.

*America. 88:668. Mr. 21, '53. Fight on banning objectionable books; editorial.

America. 90:37. Ja. 9, '54. Catholic participation in UNESCO.

American Association of University Professors Bulletin. 34:135-6. Spring '48. Statement adopted by Association of American Colleges, American Association of Teachers Colleges, American Association of University Professors, American Library Association, Association of American Law Schools, and American Political Science Association. '41 to '47.

*American Legion Magazine. 50:18+. Ja. '51. Why you buy books that sell communism. I. C. Kuhn.

*American Library Association Bulletin. 42:285. Jl.-Ag. '48. Library bill of rights.

American Library Association Bulletin. 42:599-600. D. '48. What are we afraid of? some notes on censorship. L. K. Martin.
    Same. Education Digest. 14:12-13. F. '49; *Excerpts.* National Education Association Journal. 38:252. Ap. '49.

*American Library Association Bulletin. 46:105-10. Ap. '52. Reply to Carlson. E. S. Earle.

American Mercury. 70:239-44. Jl. '53. On the free society. John Chamberlain.

*American Mercury. 78:3-8. F. '54. UNESCO, UN's brain-washing apparatus. H. L. Varney.

*American Scholar. 20, no4:396-405. Autumn '51. If anybody wants to know; address before Americans for Democratic Action, Jersey City, N.J., February 20, 1951. Mark Van Doren.

American Scholar. 22, no4:393-8. Autumn '53; 23, no 1:25-6. Winter '53-'54. Loyalty and freedom. Archibald MacLeish.

American Scholar. 23, no 1:9-25. Winter '53-'54. Some observations on intellectual freedom. David Riesman.

Bulletin of Bibliography. 20:188-91. My. '52. Selective bibliography of literary censorship in the United States. A. L. Fessler.

Catholic World. 177:241-5. Jl. '53. Sex and censorship. J. B. Sheerin.

Christian Century. 69:1169. O. 8, '52. Book burning in Alabama.

Christian Century. 70:373. Ap. 1, '53. Sex and the book publishers.

*Christian Century. 70:404. Ap. 8, '53. Vigilante censorship is spreading.

Christian Century. 70:1211-12. O. 21, '53. UNESCO cleared of false charges. W. T. Thorkelson.

*Christian Herald. p 17-18+. S. '50. America's schoolbook scandal. Clara Stilwell, pseud.

*Christian Herald. p 21-22+. My. '52. Smut on our newsstands. J. A. Kugelmass.

Clearing House. 25:491-3. Ap. '51. Time's up! School people must battle thought control. W. N. McGowan.
    Same. Education Digest. 17:1-2. S. '51.

Columbia Law Review. 53:620-31. My. '53. Speech: public and private. M. L. Ernst and A. J. Katz.

Commentary. 10:530-40. D. '50. Scarsdale's battle of the books; how one community dealt with subversive literature. Robert Shaplen.

*Commentary. 13:99-106. F. '52. What to do about 'dangerous' textbooks. E. N. Saveth.

Commonweal. 51:429. Ja. 27, '50. Censorship.

*Commonweal. 58:193-4. My. 29, '53. Sex and censorship.

Commonweal. 58:263. Je. 19, '53. Branding of the books.

Commonweal. 58:481-2. Ag. 21, '53. Who is tainted?

*Commonweal. 58:505. Ag. 28, '53. Due process.

Commonweal. 58:515-20. Ag. 28, '53. Commonweal and McCarthyism. Philip Burnham; with reply by editors.

Educational Leadership. 6:104-8. N. '48. On keeping our reading free. D. K. Berninghausen.

Educational Leadership. 10:26-30. O. '52. Use of slanted materials in the classroom. S. P. Wronski.

Educational Record. 29:392-9. O. '48. Freedom of communication within the nation. J. A. Brandt.

*Educational Record. 34:279-304. O. '53. Can textbooks be subversive? W. E. Spaulding.
    Also separate. 8p. American Textbook Publishers Institute. 1 Madison Ave. New York 10. '53.

Educational Reviewer. 1:1. Jl. 15, '49. Declaration; statement of purposes of founders of the magazine.

*Educational Reviewer. 1:3. Jl. 15, '49. Broadcasting collectivist propaganda. Edna Lonigan.
> *Same condensed.* In Cary, S. F. New challenges to our schools. 214p. (Reference Shelf. v25, no 1) H. W. Wilson Co. New York. '53.

Educational Reviewer. 1:1-7. O. 29, '49. Case against Magruder's *American Government.*

Educational Reviewer. 5:2. O. '53. Goodbye; valedictory of editors of the magazine.

Freeman. 2:142-5. D. 3, '51. Slow poison for the young idea; two educators report on pro-Soviet text [brief reports on current materials for use in education]. Felix Wittmer and T. F. Hunt.

*Freeman. 2:239-42. Ja. 14, '52. Slanted guide to library selections. Oliver Carlson.

Harper's Magazine. 200:27-30. F. '50. Easy chair: year-end megrims. Bernard De Voto.

Harper's Magazine. 206:42-5. Ap. '53. Easy chair: case of the censorious congressmen. Bernard De Voto.

*Harper's Magazine. 207:53-6. Jl. '53. How red was the red decade? Granville Hicks.

Independent Woman. 31:2-4+. Ja. '52. Let's find the truth—then stick to our course. K. F. Scott.

Independent Woman. 32:204-6+. Je. '53. Are we getting our money's worth from UNESCO? S. T. Hughes.

Journal of Public Law (Emory University Law School, Georgia) 1:303-6. What should be the relation of morals to law? M. L. Ernst.
> *Same.* 4p. The author. 285 Madison Ave. New York. '53.

Library Journal. 74:917-19. Je. 15, '49. We will gamble on the American. J. A. Ford.

Library Journal. 75:262. F. 15, '50. Intellectual trust vs. suppression in libraries. C. F. Ransom.

Library Journal. 75:652-5. Ap. 15, '50. Censorship and the immature. G. L. Schmitt.

Library Journal. 76:1071-3. Jl. '51. Frontiers of freedom; library bill of rights. D. K. Berninghausen.

*Library Journal. 76:1170-1. Ag. '51. Book selection policies. R. A. Ulveling.

*Library Journal. 76:2063. D. 15, '51. Book selection policies; keep calm and support the library bill of rights. Thurston Taylor.

*Library Journal. 76:2064-5. D. 15, '51. Book selection policies; don't split collections. Paul Bixler.

*Library Journal. 77:1927-30. N. '52. Congress as censor. E. M. Oboler.

*Library Journal. 78:1179-82. Jl. '53. Books on trial in Texas. Marie Halpenny.

Library Journal. 78:1359-65. S. 1, '53. Printed word. J. R. Wiggins.

Library Journal. 78:1616. O. 1, '53. Important ruling in Youngstown case.

*Library Journal. 79:20-5. Ja. 1, '54. United States libraries. S.D. Nerboso.

Library Trends. 2:146-70. Jl. '53. Aid to national policy. Dan Lacy.

Life. 34:32. Je. 29, '53. Books, words and deeds.

McCall's. 80:56+. O. '52. Danger's ahead in public schools. John Bainbridge.

*Midland Schools. 67:12-13+. O. '52. What about those attacks on UNESCO? R. H. Wagner.

Nation. 160:415-17. Ap. 14, '45. Censors in the saddle. Eric Sevareid.

Nation. 168:686+ Je. 18, '49. What's wrong with UNESCO? Stephen Spender.

Nation. 171:485. N. 25, '50. Dangerous thoughts; this property is condemned; the morals clause.

Nation. 173:20-2. S. 15, '51. Screening public school textbooks in Indiana.

Nation. 173:20-2. S. 15, '51. Shape of things: labeling literature.

Nation. 174:619-24. Je. 28, '52. Battle of the books. Matthew Josephson.

Nation. 174:625-8. Je. 28, '52. Behind the asbestos curtain.

Nation. 175:30-1. Jl. 12, '52. Freedom in book and classroom.

Nation. 175:[inside cover]. S. 20, '52. Hubbub over UNESCO. S. B. Haines.

Nation. 175:228-30. S. 20, '52. Campaign against the UN. Richard Friedlich.

Nation. 176:367-8. My. 2, '53. Books are burning. William Murray.

Nation. 176:515, 525. Je. 20, '53. Texas brand in the library; with editorial comment. Maury Maverick, Jr.

Nation. 177:326-30. O. 24, '53. Will they wreck the UN? Mark Gayn.

Nation. 178:26-8. Ja. 9, '54. Minute women; daughters of vigilantism. R. S. O'Leary.

Nation. 178:30-2. Ja. 9, '54. Revolt against reason. Martin Hall.

National Business Education Quarterly. 21:68-71. O. '52. Textbook publishing and distribution in America. L. W. King.

National Education Association Journal. 42:207-10. Ap. '53. Freedom of the mind. A. E. Meyer.

National Education Association Journal. 42:227-8. Ap. '53. Battle of the books. J. H. Haefner.

National Education Association Journal. 42:467. N. '53. UNESCO not Communist-dominated, committee finds.

National Parent-Teacher. 45:1. My. '51. Two principles for the use of documents critical of the schools, stated by Anna H. Hayes, president of the National Congress of Parents and Teachers.

National Parent-Teacher. 47:10-13. Ap. '53. Who's behind the textbook business? Committee on School Education. National Congress of Parents and Teachers.
> *Same condensed.* Education Digest. 18:13-15. My. '53.

National Parent-Teacher. 47:25-7. My. '53. How textbooks are made. Committee on School Education. National Congress of Parents and Teachers.
> *Also separate.* What do you know about textbooks? 11p. National Parent-Teacher. 700 N. Rush St. Chicago 11. '53.

National Parent-Teacher. 47:7-10. Je. '53. Johnny's textbooks: how good are they?
> *Also separate.* What do you know about textbooks? 11p. National Parent-Teacher. 700 N. Rush St. Chicago 11. '53.

National Parent-Teacher. 48:13-14. O. '53. What's happening in education? What about self-appointed vigilantes? W. D. Boutwell.

National Republic. 69:13-15+. Je. '53. Initiators of operation socialism. Felix Wittmer.

New Republic. 125:14-15. O. 29, '51. Techniques of intimidation. A. J. Heidenheimer.

New Republic. 126:7-17. Je. 29, '52. Special report on book burning.
> *Also separate.* 13p. New Republic. 1826 Jefferson Pl. N.W. Washington 6, D.C. '52.

*New Republic. 127:11-13. Jl. 14, '52. Legion and the library. L. P. Beth.
> *Reply with rejoinder.* H. C. Wolf. 127:2+. Ag. 11, '52.

New Republic. 127:5. S. 7, '52. Firefighting.

New Republic. 127:7. S. 22, '52. Pressures in Los Angeles.

New Republic. 128:9. Ap. 6, '53. Perils of compromise; directive to U.S. libraries overseas.

New Republic. 129:3. Ag. 31, '53. Texas test.

New York Times. p33. O. 26, '48. Supreme Court tie vote upholds New York State court conviction of Doubleday & Co., Hecate County Memoirs obscenity case.

New York Times. p 1. O. 12, '52. State [New York] still awaits red text charges.
> *Also separate.* 1p. American Textbook Publishers Institute. 1 Madison Ave. New York 10. '52.

New York Times. p E8. Mr. 1, '53. Ban on books explained. Letter to the editor. E. J. Allen.

New York Times. p E8. Mr. 8, '53. Book ban protested. Letter to the editor. Victor Weybright.

*New York Times. p 16. Jl. 1, '53. Dulles' aides cite 'mission' on books. W. H. Waggoner.

*New York Times. p 1+. N. 14, '53. Indiana censor fears little Red Robin Hood.

New York Times Magazine. p 11+. Jl. 12, '53. Book branding, case history. Stanley Walker.

New Yorker. 25:19. O. 8, '49. Board of Education criteria for selecting textbooks, library books, and magazines for use in public schools.

Newsweek. 41:23. Je. 29, '53. Something burning? book burners.

Newsweek. 42:25. Jl. 6, '53. Whaddaya read?

Ohio Library Association Bulletin. 22:3-4. F. '52. Letter to members of the Intellectual Freedom Committee of the Ohio Library Association. Paul Bixler.

*Parents' Magazine. 27:46+. D. '52. Truth about textbook censorship. Benjamin Fine.

Phi Delta Kappan. 30:281-2. Mr. '49. Promote the free flow of information. Milton Eisenhower.

Phi Delta Kappan. 33:1-300. Ja. '52. Textbooks and the schools [entire issue].

Publishers' Weekly. 155:1512-13, 19. Ap. 2, '49. Judge Bok clears nine novels involved in Pennsylvania trial; summary of opinion involving definition of obscenity in literature, with editorial comment.

Publishers' Weekly. 157:1691. Ap. 8, '50. No letup in fight against book banning. F. G. Melcher.

Publishers' Weekly. 157:1885-7. Ap. 29, '50. Censorship through the open market rather than the police station. Curtis Bok.

Publishers' Weekly. 160:1381-3. S. 29, '51. Defenders of books and public schools analyze recent attacks.

Publishers' Weekly. 162:2240-1. D. 6, '52. Censorship plans urged at paper-book hearings.

Publishers' Weekly. 162:2321. D. 13, '52. Editors and teachers attack textbook censors.

*Publishers' Weekly. 163:1058-60. F. 28, '53. Book censorship is reaching epidemic proportions.

Publishers' Weekly. 163:1062. F. 28, '53. Colonel Voorhees convicted in army court-martial.

*Publishers' Weekly. 163:1511-13. Ap. 4, '53. Attack on books; a publisher's analysis. Victor Weybright.

*Publishers' Weekly. 163:2384-6. Je. 6, '53. American public trusts the bookseller. E. A. Weeks.

Saturday Review. 35:14-24+. Ap. 19, '52. Textbook problem (symposium). F. M. Hechinger and others.
    Discussion. 35:21-2. My. 17, '52; 24. Jl. 26, '52.

*Saturday Review. 35:22-3. S. 6, '52. Censors and the public. W. D. Patterson.

*Saturday Review. 36:27-8. Jl. 11, '53. Duty of freedom. C. L. Bok.

Saturday Review. 36:29+. Jl. 11, '53. Enclaves of America overseas. W. C. Haygood.

*Saturday Review. 36:30-1. Jl. 11, '53. Open the books. Norman Cousins.

Saturday Review of Literature. 32:9-10. F. 26, '49. Sensitivity as censor: attitudes of American minority groups. J. H. Holmes.
  Discussion. 32:23-4. Mr. 19, '49; 23-4. Mr. 26, '49; 31-2. Ap. 16, '49; 9-10. Ap. 30, '49; 23-5. My. 7, '49.
Saturday Review of Literature. 32:28. Ap. 16, '49. Censorship can be stopped; with summary of Judge Bok's opinion in Philadelphia trial. Harrison Smith.
Saturday Review of Literature. 32:22. My. 28, '49. Censorship controversy. Norman Cousins.
Saturday Review of Literature. 33:9-10+. F. 25, '50. Reading by red star light. J. P. MacCormac.
Saturday Review of Literature. 33:25. Ap. 1, '50. Free expression in U.S.A. Elmer Rice.
School and Society. 48:405-7. S. 24, '38. Should school books be censored?
School and Society. 70:792-3. D. 10, '49. Loyalty to freedom; scrutinizing school textbooks. J. S. Brubacher.
School and Society. 74:345-6. D. 1, '51. Who shall write unbiased textbooks. P. H. Epps.
School and Society. 78:43-4. Ag. 8, '53. Freedom of reading and the future of democracy. I. L. Kandel.
School Life. 32:49-51. Ja. '50. UNESCO: is it going our way? G. D. Stoddard.
Senior Scholastic. 55:47. N. 2, '49. Business brass wades into Scarsdale book battle.
Senior Scholastic. 60:5-7. F. 20, '52. Does UNESCO point the path to peace; New York Times youth forum discussion.
Social Education. 15:234-5. My. '51. Statement by National Council for Social Studies.
Social Education. 17:65-70. F. '53. Freedom to learn: censorship in learning materials. T. K. Serviss.
Social Education. 17:165-70. Ap. '53. Freedom to learn: censorship and learning materials. M. R. Ahrens.
Social Studies. 40:178-9. Ap. '49. Group pressure and censorship. L. B. Irwin.
Survey. 88:112-15. Mr. '52. New fashions in censorship by special-interest pressure groups. Elmer Rice.
  Reply with rejoinder. Survey. 88:148. Ap. '52.
Time. 59:72-4. My. 5, '52. Creeping censorship.
Time. 61:65. Mr. 9, '53. All lustful; censorship in Georgia.
Time. 61:34+. Je. 22, '53. Verboten volumes; Amerika häuser.
Time. 63.98. Ja. 18, '54. It didn't happen here.
Town Meeting (Bulletin of America's Town Meeting of the Air). 17, no 46:1-14. Mr. 11, '52. Do critics and reviewers have too much influence? J. B. Brown, Ilka Chase, Orville Prescott, Dr. Houston Peterson, moderator.
United Nations Bulletin. 10:210-13. Mr. 1, '51. Draft convention on freedom of information.

United States News & World Report. 34:37-40 +. Je. 26, '53. Book burning: where U.S. officials stand.

University of Chicago Round Table. 795:1-18. Jl. 5, '53. Book burning and censorship. Harry Kalven, Jr., K. N. Llewellyn, Robert Faulhaber.

*Vital Speeches of the Day. 19:570-1. Jl. 1, '53. Fun and courage. D. D. Eisenhower.

Wilson Library Bulletin. 27:790. Je. '53. Minnesota censorship bill defeated. E. B. Stanford.

Wilson Library Bulletin. 27:807-12. Je. '53. Attack on books in libraries; report of a library public relations council meeting on censorship.

*Wilson Library Bulletin. 28:59-60. S. '53. President Eisenhower on freedom to read; letter from the White House to the American Library Association.

  Also separate. 4p. H. W. Wilson Co. New York. '53.

*Wilson Library Bulletin. 28:60-2. S. '53. Freedom to read; statement prepared by Westchester Conference of American Library Association and American Book Publishers Council—May 2 and 3, 1953.

  Same. Saturday Review. 36:24-7. Jl. 11, '53; *Same with editorial comment.* Library Journal. 78:1272-5. Ag. '53; *Same abridged.* New Republic. 128:5-6. Jl. 6, '53. Time. 62:62-4. Jl. 6, '53; *Also separate.* 4p. H. W. Wilson Co. New York. '53.

*Wilson Library Bulletin. 28:63-8. S. '53. Not censorship but selection; address by Lester Asheim before International Freedom Conference, Whittier, California, June 1953.

Yale Law Journal. 61:295-333. Mr. '52. Security measures and freedom of thought. Marie Jahoda and S. W. Cook.